C000264306

Wallace & Gromit™
Cracking Celebration Cakes

Based on characters created by Nick Park

Debbie Brown

Dedication

This book is dedicated to my true friend and mentor, Elaine.
Thank you for making the world a better place.

Acknowledgements

The author would like to thank:

Alister for his amazing photography

Jenny and Sarah for their warmth, enthusiasm and total professionalism

Renshaw for supplying high quality Regalice sugarpaste used throughout this book

Wallace & Gromit™

Cracking Celebration Cakes

First published in
September 2006 by
B. Dutton Publishing Limited,
Alfred House,
Hones Business Park,
Farnham, Surrey,
GU9 8BB, UK.

ISBN-10: 1-905113-04-8

ISBN-13: 978-1-905113-04-0

**Copyright © and TM. Aardman Animations
Limited 2006. All Rights Reserved. Wallace
and Gromit (word mark) and the
characters "Wallace" and "Gromit" © and
TM Aardman Wallace and Gromit Limited.**

Text and cake design: Debra Brown 2006

Typography and photography:
B. Dutton Publishing Limited 2006

All rights reserved.

No part of this publication may be
reproduced, stored in a retrieval system or
transmitted in any form or by means
electronic, mechanical, photocopying,
recording, or otherwise, without prior written
permission of the copyright owner. A
catalogue record of this book is available
from the British Library.

Debra Brown has asserted her right under
the Copyright, Designs and Patents Act,
1988, to be identified as the
author of this work.

Publisher: Beverley Dutton

Editor: Jenny Stewart

Designer: Sarah Richardson

Editorial Assistant: Clare Porter

Design Assistant: Zena Manicom

Photography: Alister Thorpe

Printed in Slovenia by arrangement
with Associated Agencies Limited

Introduction

Capturing the essence of Wallace and Gromit in cake and sugar has been quite fascinating and definitely enjoyable. They are such interesting characters with their quintessentially British personalities and the antics they both get up to that I found a plethora of material to inspire cake designs. It was certainly a challenge to narrow down ideas and I could've filled this book twice over!

Wallace's fantastic, highly detailed inventions gave me plenty of ideas for interesting cake designs. Some were a little too complicated and time consuming to be suitable for cake decoration, so I chose to make the simpler inventions that could easily be reproduced as a cake sculpture or sugar model and have put together this varied collection of fun cakes suitable for many special celebrations.

There is a cake here to suit everyone, from beginner to experienced cake decorator. All the cakes are within everyone's capabilities, each one achievable within a sensible time frame. If you are short of time, there are several designs that can be completed in an hour or so; other cakes are more involved but worth spending a little more time creating something spectacular. Whichever project you choose to make, follow the instructions and you will find that, when the cake is complete, you have a fantastic centrepiece that will amaze and delight everyone, making the celebration unforgettable.

Debbie

Contents

Recipes

Madeira Sponge Cake

This recipe is moist and light, but still suitable for carving and sculpting without crumbling. I would recommend using this recipe in preference to shop-bought cake mixes as when baked, these can be too soft and crumbly to withstand being sculpted into different shapes. For intricately sculpted cakes or cakes with height, use the amount of plain flour stated in the baking chart. To make a lighter cake suitable for simpler designs, you may slightly reduce the amount of plain flour.

Please refer to the Baking Chart (see pages 14 to 15) for the ingredient quantities, cake tin sizes and baking times for each project.

Tip

To settle and limit the crust on the top of the cake and also keep the cake as moist as possible, place a baking sheet or a sheet of foil over the top of the bakeware during baking. When the cake is baked, leave the sheet on top of the tin when removed from the oven until the cake has cooled and is ready to turn out.

Method

1. Preheat the oven to 150°C/325°F/Gas Mark 3. Grease and line the bakeware.

2. Sift the self-raising and plain/all-purpose flour together in a bowl.

3. Soften the butter and put it in a food mixer or large mixing bowl with the caster/superfine sugar. Beat until the mixture is pale and fluffy.

4. Add the eggs to the mixture one at a time with a spoonful of the sifted flour, beating well after each addition. Add the vanilla essence/flavouring.

5. Using a spatula or large spoon, fold the remaining flour into the mixture.

6. Spoon the mixture into the bakeware, and then make a dip in the top of the mixture using the back of a spoon.

7. Bake in the centre of the oven until a skewer inserted in the centre comes out clean.

8. When baked, remove the cake from the oven and leave to cool in the bakeware for five minutes, then turn out onto a wire rack and leave to cool completely. When cold, store in an airtight container or double wrap in clingfilm (plastic food wrap) for at least eight hours, allowing the texture to settle before use.

Basic variations for Madeira cake:

Chocolate marble cake

Before spooning the cake mixture into the bakeware, fold in 200g (7oz) of melted chocolate until marbled. The chocolate can be folded in completely for a light chocolate cake.

Chocolate orange marble cake

Add melted chocolate, as for the chocolate marble cake, and add the grated rind and juice of 1 organic orange.

Lemon cake

Add the grated rind and juice of 1 organic lemon to the cake mixture.

Coffee cake

Add 30ml (2tbsp) of coffee essence to the cake mixture.

Almond cake

Add 4ml (1tsp) of almond essence and 30-45ml (2-3tbsp) of ground almonds to the cake mixture.

Buttercream

Buttercream is a versatile icing used as a cake filling, to crumb-coat cakes (sealing the cake to stop it drying out), and to adhere the sugarpaste coating to a cake. For intricately sculpted cakes, leave the crumb coat to set firmly, then add a little more buttercream or rework the surface using a palette knife dipped into warm water to soften the buttercream so the sugarpaste will stick to the cake.

Makes approximately 625g (1lb 6oz)

Ingredients

175g (6oz) unsalted butter, softened

10-15ml (2-3tbsp) milk

5ml (1tsp) vanilla essence

450g (1lb) icing (confectioner's) sugar, sifted

Method

1. Place the softened butter, milk and essence into a mixer. Add the icing sugar a little at a time, mixing on medium speed, until light, fluffy and pale in colour.

2. Store in an airtight container and use within ten days. Bring to room temperature and beat again before use.

Basic variations for buttercream:

Chocolate

Add 90g (3oz) of good quality melted chocolate, or use 45-60ml (3-4 level tbsp) of cocoa powder mixed to a paste with milk.

Orange

Add 30-45ml (2-3 level tbsp) of orange or lemon curd.

Coffee

Add 30-45ml (2-3tbsp) of coffee essence.

Raspberry

Add 30-45ml (2-3 level tbsp) of seedless raspberry jam.

Almond

Add 5ml (1tsp) of almond essence.

Sugarpaste (Rolled Fondant)

I have used Renshaw's Regalice sugarpaste throughout this book as it is a good quality brand and is easy to use. Sugarpaste (sometimes known as rolled fondant) is readily available throughout the UK in supermarkets and cake decorating outlets. Each brand has a slightly different texture, taste and working quality, so try different brands to find which suits you best. If you prefer to make your own, I would recommend the recipe below.

Makes 625g (1lb 6oz)

Ingredients

1 egg white made up from dried egg albumen

30ml (2tbsp) liquid glucose

625g (1lb 6oz) icing (confectioner's) sugar

A little white vegetable fat/shortening, if required

A pinch of CMC*

* NOTE: CMC is an abbreviation of Carboxy Methyl Cellulose, an edible thickener widely used in the food industry. The CMC you use must be food grade. Brand names include SK CMC, Tylose, Tylopur, Tylo and Sugarcel. Alternatively, you can use SK Gum Tragacanth, which is a natural product.

Tip

To save time when decorating a cake, homemade sugarpaste can be frozen for up to three months.

Method

1. Put the egg white and liquid glucose into a bowl, using a warm spoon for the liquid glucose.

2. Sift the icing sugar into the bowl, adding a little at a time and stirring until the mixture thickens.

3. Turn the mixture out onto a work surface dusted liberally with icing sugar and knead the paste until soft, smooth and pliable. If the paste is slightly dry and cracked, fold in a little white vegetable fat and knead again. If the paste is very soft and sticky, add a little more icing sugar. Add a pinch of CMC to strengthen the paste.

4. Transfer the paste immediately into a food-grade polythene bag and store in an airtight container. Keep the paste cool, either at room temperature, or in the refrigerator if the atmosphere is warm. Bring back to room temperature and knead thoroughly before use.

Royal Icing

Royal icing is used to pipe fine details and to stick sugar pieces together as when dry it will hold items firmly in place. Ready-made royal icing can be obtained from supermarkets or in powder form (follow instructions on the packet). If you prefer to make your own, you can follow this recipe.

Makes 75g (2$^1/_2$oz)

Ingredients

5ml (1 level tsp) egg albumen

15ml (3tsp) cooled, boiled water

65-70g (2$^1/_4$oz) icing sugar

Method

1. Put the egg albumen into a bowl. Add the water and stir until dissolved.

2. Beat in the icing sugar a little at a time until the icing is firm, glossy and forms peaks if a spoon is pulled out.

3. To stop the icing forming a crust, place a damp cloth over the top of the bowl until you are ready to use it or transfer to an airtight container and refrigerate.

Edible Glue

This recipe makes a strong sugar glue which works extremely well. Alternatively, ready-made sugar glue can be purchased from specialist cake decorating outlets.

Ingredients

1.25ml ($^1/_4$tsp) CMC powder

30ml (2tbsp) boiled water, cooled until warm

Method

1. Mix the CMC powder with warm water and leave to stand until the powder has fully dissolved. The glue should be smooth and have a soft dropping consistency. If the glue thickens after a few days, add a few more drops of water.

2. Store in an airtight container in the refrigerator and use within one week.

3. To use, brush a thin coat over the surface of the item you wish to glue, leave for a few moments to become tacky, and then press the item in place.

11

Modelling Paste

This quick and easy recipe makes a high quality modelling paste. If you are short of time or prefer to use a ready-made paste, SK Mexican Modelling Paste is ready-to-use and is available in several colours, including Flesh, which is ideal for Wallace.

Ingredients

450g (1lb) Renshaw's Regalice sugarpaste

5ml (1 level tsp) CMC powder

Method

Knead the CMC into the sugarpaste. The sugarpaste will start to thicken as soon as CMC is incorporated so can be used immediately. The paste will continue to thicken gradually over a period of 24 hours. The amount of CMC can be varied depending on usage and on the room temperature, atmospheric conditions, etc., so adjust accordingly to achieve the required consistency. Store in an airtight container.

NOTE: The amount of CMC used can be varied depending on the room temperature, humidity and your preference for stiffness of paste.

Quick Pastillage

Pastillage is a fast-drying paste which dries extremely hard and will keep its shape. It is suitable for items like the Were-rabbit's silhouette (see page 55). Like royal icing, ready-made powder mixes are available from sugarcraft shops.

Makes 260g (9oz) pastillage

Ingredients

260g (9oz) royal icing, made to stiff peak consistency

10ml (2 level tsp) CMC powder

Icing sugar in shaker

Method

1. Mix the CMC into the stiff peak royal icing. The mixture will thicken immediately. Knead on a work surface sprinkled liberally with icing sugar until the mixture forms a paste and is smooth and crack-free.

2. Keep the pastillage airtight and store in a refrigerator. Bring back to room temperature before use.

NOTE: The amount of CMC used can be varied depending on the room temperature, humidity and your preference for stiffness of paste.

Sugar Sticks

These are cut or rolled lengths of pastillage and are used as edible supports, mainly to help hold modelled heads in place. If you are short of time, you can use strands of dried, raw spaghetti, but remember to remove them before the figures are eaten.

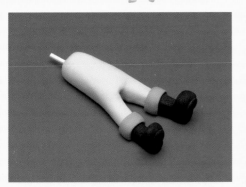

Makes around 10-20 sugar sticks

Ingredients

5ml (1 level tsp) royal icing, made to stiff peak consistency

1.25ml (¼tsp) CMC

Icing sugar in sugar shaker

Method

1. Knead the CMC into the royal icing until the mixture thickens and forms a paste. If the paste is slightly wet, knead in a little icing sugar until the paste is soft and pliable.

2. Either roll out the paste and cut into different sized strips of various lengths using a plain-bladed knife, or roll individual sausages of paste to the sizes required. Leave to dry, preferably overnight on a sheet of food-grade foam. When completely dry, store in an airtight container.

Baking Chart

This chart gives the baking tin sizes, quantities of ingredients and suggested baking times required to make all the cakes featured in this book. Full instructions for making each cake, including oven temperatures, and further recipe ideas are given on pages 8 to 9.

Project	Bakeware	Ingredients		Baking time
Bunnies Everywhere	20cm (8") and 13cm (5") round tins	Unsalted butter, softened Caster/superfine sugar Large eggs Self-raising flour Plain/all-purpose flour	400g (14oz) 400g (14oz) 7 400g (14oz) 200g (7oz)	$1^1/_4$–$1^1/_2$ hours
Gromit's Bathtime	23cm x 18cm (9" x 7") oval-shaped tin and 25cm (10") round tin	Unsalted butter, softened Caster/superfine sugar Large eggs Self-raising flour Plain/all-purpose flour	450g (1lb) 450g (1lb) 8 450g (1lb) 225g (8oz)	1–$1^1/_4$ hours
Anti-pesto Van	28cm (11") square tin	Unsalted butter, softened Caster/superfine sugar Large eggs Self-raising flour Plain/all-purpose flour	340g (12oz) 340g (12oz) 6 340g (12oz) 175g (6oz)	1–$1^1/_4$ hours
Pop Art	2 x 15cm (6") square tins	Unsalted butter, softened Caster/superfine sugar Large eggs Self-raising flour Plain/all-purpose flour	340g (12oz) 340g (12oz) 6 340g (12oz) 175g (6oz)	$1^1/_4$–$1^1/_2$ hours
Mini Cakes	5cm (2") cube tin set (mixture for 12 sections)	Unsalted butter, softened Caster/superfine sugar Large eggs Self-raising flour Plain/all-purpose flour	175g (6oz) 175g (6oz) 3 175g (6oz) 90g (3oz)	30–40 minutes
Beware the Were-rabbit	20cm (8") and 15cm (6") square tins	Unsalted butter, softened Caster/superfine sugar Large eggs Self-raising flour Plain/all-purpose flour	400g (14oz) 400g (14oz) 7 400g (14oz) 200g (7oz)	1–$1^1/_4$ hours

Project	Bakeware	Ingredients		Baking time
Anyone for Football? Rocket to the Moon	2 x 1 litre (2 pint) ovenproof bowls or 1 x spherical tin	Unsalted butter, softened Caster/superfine sugar Large eggs Self-raising flour Plain/all-purpose flour	285g (10oz) 285g (10oz) 5 285g (10oz) 145g (5oz)	$1^1/_4$ hours
Wallace Through the Porthole!	25cm (10") round tin	Unsalted butter, softened Caster/superfine sugar Large eggs Self-raising flour Plain/all-purpose flour	340g (12oz) 340g (12oz) 6 340g (12oz) 175g (6oz)	$1^1/_4$–$1^1/_2$ hours
Train Chase Crackers about Cheese	20cm (8") round tin	Unsalted butter, softened Caster/superfine sugar Large eggs Self-raising flour Plain/all-purpose flour	225g (8oz) 225g (8oz) 4 225g (8oz) 115g (4oz)	1–$1^1/_4$ hours
Dogfight Knit One, Purl One	25cm (10") square tin	Unsalted butter, softened Caster/superfine sugar Large eggs Self-raising flour Plain/all-purpose flour	340g (12oz) 340g (12oz) 6 340g (12oz) 175g (6oz)	$1^1/_4$–$1^1/_2$ hours
Gromit	25cm x 15cm (10" x 6") oblong tin and 1 litre (2 pint) ovenproof bowl or $^1/_2$ spherical tin	Unsalted butter, softened Caster/superfine sugar Large eggs Self-raising flour Plain/all-purpose flour	340g (12oz) 340g (12oz) 6 340g (12oz) 175g (6oz)	1–$1^1/_2$ hours
Gromit's Christmas Kennel The Flying Sidecar Tea Time The Great British Sandcastle	30cm (12") square tin	Unsalted butter, softened Caster/superfine sugar Large eggs Self-raising flour Plain/all-purpose flour	340g (12oz) 340g (12oz) 6 340g (12oz) 175g (6oz)	1 hour
Rabbit Hunt	20cm (8") square tin	Unsalted butter, softened Caster/superfine sugar Large eggs Self-raising flour Plain/all-purpose flour	285g (10oz) 285g (10oz) 5 285g (10oz) 145g (5oz)	$1^1/_4$–$1^1/_2$ hours
Paw Print Cupcakes	12-hole bun tin	Unsalted butter, softened Caster/superfine sugar Large eggs Self-raising flour Plain/all-purpose flour	115g (4oz) 115g (4oz) 2 115g (4oz) 60g (2oz)	20–30 minutes

Techniques and Equipment

Basic Equipment

There is an extensive choice of tools and equipment available for cake decorating and sugar modelling, from any shape of cutter you can imagine to embossers that can be used to create any type of texture or pattern you could ever need. They help to inspire, and of course save time, as these aids do some of the work for you. Although there are many of these specialist items on the market, most projects throughout this book only require basic materials and equipment. Where particular details are featured on a cake, I have explained how to obtain the required result without having to purchase several specialist items. However, you may prefer to invest in some of these tools if you are an avid sugarcrafter.

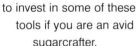

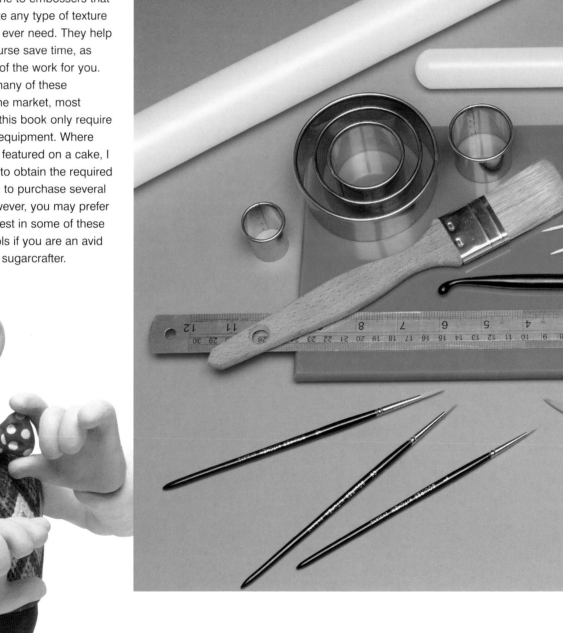

- Large and small rolling pins: ideally, you should have one that is large enough to roll out sugarpaste for covering cakes without leaving marks, and a smaller one for detailed work. Choose food-safe polypropylene rolling pins as the surface is exceptionally smooth so won't mark the paste and is easy to clean.

- Non-stick board: although you can successfully roll out paste on a clean work surface, I would recommend using a large non-stick polypropylene work board for convenience.

- Small, straight-bladed vegetable knife: you will need a knife for cutting sugarpaste and modelling paste. Make sure that the blade isn't too thick and heavy and that the handle doesn't impede cutting.

- Medium-sized serrated knife: this is perfect for sculpting the surface of cakes as it slices through the cake easily without breaking pieces off.

- Turntable: although this is not a necessity, I always recommend using a turntable. It not only elevates your work to eye level, it also allows you to work on all areas of the cake without handling it too much, thus minimising marks on the surface of the cake.

- Cake smoother: an essential tool for smoothing out any uneven surfaces in paste, particularly when covering a cake.

- Food-grade foam: this is invaluable for supporting your modelled pieces in position whilst they dry.

- Pastry brush: this is ideal for dampening cake boards before they are covered with sugarpaste and the large bristles make it useful for creating paint effects.

Other equipment that I would recommend you have to hand is a sugar shaker for dusting your work area with icing sugar, a ruler, good quality sable paintbrushes, a ball tool or bone tool, cocktail sticks, a scourer or texture mat and a set of circle cutters, from miniature through to cookie size or even larger (remember though that there are many items in your kitchen cupboards that you can cut around, from little pot lids to cups and saucers). Keep all your equipment in a separate container solely for sugarcraft use to ensure it is kept clean and is safe for food use, particularly paintbrushes, rulers, pot scourers, etc.

Cake Sculpting

Always remove the crust from the cake as this can be loose after the buttercream and sugarpaste have been applied to the surface. If the crust is loose, it may cause the covering to pull away, especially if a heavy item is glued against it. Removing the crust also makes the cake easier to sculpt.

To sculpt a cake, use a serrated knife to cut away a little at a time, shaving off small pieces until you have the required shape. If you cut off more than you need

to, you can stick pieces of cake back on with a little buttercream (try not to do this too much as it may cause the sugarpaste to slip when applied).

When building up a high cake like the Were-rabbit sculpture (see page 87), make sure that each layer is completely straight and that the cake is well balanced. If part of the cake is left only slightly uneven it will look much worse when covered with sugarpaste and may cause the cake to lean.

How to Cover a Cake

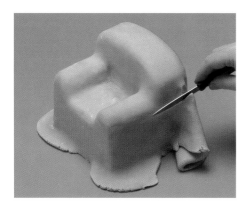

When you have carved and crumb-coated a cake with buttercream, there are different methods for covering it with sugarpaste, depending on the shape and design of the cake. The top and sides can be covered using one piece of sugarpaste, providing that no sharp edges or corners are required. If the cake is tall, this method would make the sugarpaste too heavy and create pleats round the sides, so the top of the cake should be

covered first before a separate piece of sugarpaste is wrapped around the sides. This method is also used where a sharp, neat edge is required around the top of the cake. If sharp edges are required or a specific shape features on the cake covering, individual panels of sugarpaste can be cut for each side of the cake, using a template to ensure that you create the exact shape required.

Preparing the sugarpaste

Before covering a cake, prepare the sugarpaste covering by kneading thoroughly until it is soft and pliable. When kneading sugarpaste, do not use any icing sugar as this may cause the paste to become dry. To roll out, first sprinkle the work surface with a little icing sugar and then roll out as evenly as possible to the required size, turning the paste to loosen it

Tip

As soon as you take sugarpaste out of its airtight packaging it will start to dry, so always knead it thoroughly and then roll out or shape it as quickly as possible.

from the work surface after each roll. When using sugarpaste as a covering, roll to a thickness of 3-4mm ($1/8$"), unless stated otherwise. When ready, the texture of the sugarpaste should be soft and smooth. (If you are working in a hot climate where icing sugar could become wet and sticky, lightly grease the work surface with a little white vegetable fat instead.)

Method 1: covering the top and sides all-in-one

Projects: Rabbit Hunt, Rabbits Everywhere, The Great British Sandcastle, Hutch, Anti-pesto Van (excluding the base), Tea Time, Pop Art, Mini Cakes, Wallace, Gromit, Train Chase, Knit One, Purl One, The Flying Sidecar

This method is ideal for shapes where softened curves and edges are required (like the armchair in Knit One, Purl One, see page 91) as well as more conventional round or square cakes. Use a large rolling pin to roughly measure the cake covering area (i.e. across the top and down the sides) and roll out the paste to the required size. Place the rolling pin down onto the centre of the rolled out sugarpaste, lift the top of the sugarpaste and fold it over the rolling pin. Holding both ends of the rolling pin, lift the sugarpaste (this minimises the risk of stretching or tearing the paste) and position the sugarpaste over the top of the cake. Smooth around the shape to push out any air bubbles, and then smooth down the sides with the palm of your hand, stretching out any pleats in the paste. Trim away the excess from around the base of the cake. Rub the surface gently with a cake smoother to remove any imperfections and achieve a smooth surface. After smoothing the sides, you may need to re-trim around the base once again to create a neat edge.

Method 2: wrapping the sugarpaste around the cake

Projects: Rocket to the Moon, Gromit's Bathtime, Beware the Were-rabbit, base of Anti-pesto Van, Through the Porthole!

Roll out the kneaded sugarpaste and cut a strip to the required size, i.e. the height of the cake by the circumference. Dust the surface of the sugarpaste with icing sugar to prevent it from sticking to itself and then roll it into a spiral to help prevent the sugarpaste from stretching out of shape and tearing. Starting at the back of the cake (unless the instructions denote otherwise), place the sugarpaste against the side of the cake and unroll the paste around the shape. Trim the paste neatly at the join and smooth closed by rubbing gently with your fingers. Use a little edible glue if necessary to secure the join. The top of the cake may need to be covered separately, so follow the instructions for the project you are making.

Method 3: covering the cake using templates

Projects: Gromit's Christmas Kennel, Anyone for Football?, Dogfight

Roll out the sugarpaste to the required size and cut out the shape required using a template traced onto greaseproof paper. (You may not need a template if you are cutting the paste to the same size as the cake: carefully measure the cake with a ruler and cut the paste to size.) Carefully pick up the sugarpaste, making sure you do not mark the surface or stretch it out of shape. Position the paste against the cake and smooth the surface with a cake smoother, taking care not to distort the shape too much. You may need to re-trim the sugarpaste whilst the shape is on the cake. To straighten the edging, press along the edge with the cake smoother.

How to Cover a Cake Board

The cake board is an integral part of the cake design, so it is important to cover it with sugarpaste. Usually the cake board is covered in one piece, but some designs dictate an alternative covering, like the chequerboard floor tiles (see page 65). In this case, the individual squares of sugarpaste are carefully measured so the design works to the size of the board. To save time, you can simplify this type of design by using just one colour, covering the board in the usual way then indenting the pattern using a ruler.

To cover the cake board in one piece, first moisten the surface of the cake board slightly with a little cooled, boiled water using a pastry brush. Knead and roll out the sugarpaste to the required size (see page 18), no more than 2-3mm ($^1/_{16}$") thick. Lift the sugarpaste carefully using the rolling pin, as previously described, and position it on the cake

board. Gently roll over the top of the cake board with the rolling pin and trim away the excess paste from around the edge.

Where an uneven covering is required, such as the snowy ground in Gromit's Christmas Kennel (see page 115), position the cake on the board before rolling a strip of sugarpaste to go around the edge. Trim to fit, as before.

Dowelling a Cake

Food-safe wooden or plastic cake dowels can be used for internal support if necessary, but always make sure they are removed before serving. Tall cakes like the Were-rabbit (see page 87) and Rocket to the Moon (see page 29) could benefit from the use of an internal dowel if the atmosphere is hot and humid, as the filling softens in the heat, causing the layers to slip. For tiered cakes, such as Rabbits Everywhere (see page 105), make sure you cut all dowels evenly so the top cake sits straight. The cake card used

underneath the upper tier(s) will rest on the dowels, holding the weight and preventing the base cake from sinking or bulging.

Always ensure the dowels are evenly spaced around the central point of the cake (I usually use between three and four, depending on the size of the cakes) and are within the size and shape of the upper tier.

Working with Sugarpaste

Colouring

Some brands or recipes for sugarpaste take colour quite quickly, whilst in others that have more of an elastic consistency, it tends to take much more time for the colour to be kneaded in until there are no streaks or marbling and the colour is evenly dispersed. I find the best way to colour sugarpaste, especially deep shades, is to colour a small amount very deeply first and then knead this paste into the required amount. The colour is then dispersed into the sugarpaste much faster and more evenly.

Use a cocktail stick to add the colouring to the paste, fold the colour inside and then carefully knead the sugarpaste, taking care not to get the colouring on your hands as it can temporarily stain your skin. A little white vegetable fat rubbed into your hands first can help prevent staining; alternatively, you can protect your hands with disposable, food-safe plastic gloves.

As you knead the colour into the sugarpaste, it will create a marbled effect. Keep kneading until all the colour is dispersed evenly with no streaks. When sugarpaste is being kneaded, the colour is paler by at least one shade, so take care not to add too much colour at the start. Place the coloured sugarpaste in an airtight polythene bag and set aside to rest for a few moments to check the resulting shade is correct. For different types of colour and their application, see the Using Colour Successfully section overleaf.

Storing

To prevent sugarpaste from drying out, keep it airtight, i.e. tightly wrapped in a polythene food bag and then placed in an airtight container. Store coloured sugarpaste separately as the colours may bleed. Usually, sugarpaste should be kept at room temperature, but in extremely hot or humid conditions, store airtight in a refrigerator. Bring back to room temperature before use.

Sugarpaste can be frozen for up to three months but should be allowed to defrost thoroughly before use.

Ribbon Banding

Cake drums are often used as cake bases, particularly in the UK, and these have an edge that can be covered with ribbon to complement your cake. The ribbon used is 15mm wide, slightly deeper than the cake board to allow for the depth of the sugarpaste covering.

The easiest way to attach ribbon to the edge of a cake drum is to use a non-toxic, solid glue stick, the type usually used in paper crafts. Rub the glue stick around the cake board edge, taking care not to touch the sugarpaste edging. Starting at the back of the cake, stick the ribbon around the cake board edge, running your finger along the bottom to keep the ribbon straight. Overlap the ribbon slightly and cut off the excess at the join.

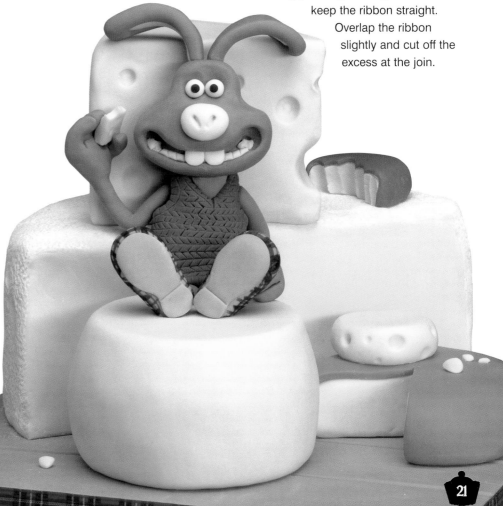

Using Colour Successfully

Food colourings are available in three main types: paste, liquid and dust (powder). They each have different uses, as described here.

Paste food colours

Paste colours are used to colour roll-out pastes such as sugarpaste, modelling paste, pastillage and marzipan as well as royal icing and buttercream. They are ideal for this purpose as they alter the consistency of the icing/paste less than dust or liquid colours. They can also be used to paint onto paste and can be diluted using a little clear alcohol or cooled, boiled water.

Paste colours are concentrated so you only need to add a tiny amount at a time until the required shade is achieved. Make sure you blend the colour well by kneading it into the paste. Coloured sugarpaste deepens on standing by at least one shade, so be careful not to use too much colour and always allow the sugarpaste to 'rest' in an airtight polythene bag before use to see the true colour.

If you require a deep colour, using large amounts of paste colour can cause the paste to become too soft and sticky. High-strength colours are ideal for this purpose

as only a small amount is required, so the consistency of the paste is not dramatically altered. You may also find certain colours can dry the paste a little, so use a little white vegetable fat on your hands to add moisture, but take care not to add too much or it may alter the consistency.

Dust food colours

Dust colours can be used to add a subtle hue to the surface of dried sugarpaste. To use, sprinkle the powder onto kitchen paper and spread out over the surface. Pick up the colour on either a dusting brush or a large sable paintbrush and apply to the paste, building up the colour in several layers if required to achieve a deeper shade.

Lustre or sparkle powders can be used in the same way to create metallic or shiny effects. For a denser colour and shine, the surface of the sugarpaste will need to be damp or sticky before the colour is applied. To achieve this, you can use

either a little edible glue spread evenly over the surface, a tiny amount of white vegetable fat or SK Gildesol, a product which has been designed for this purpose. When the lustre or sparkle powders are brushed on the surface repeatedly it will buff the surface and become shiny. Alternatively, for a more controllable way of achieving a dense lustre or sparkle, mix the powder with clear alcohol (vodka or gin, for example) to a painting consistency and paint over the surface. The alcohol will evaporate rapidly, so the colour dries quickly on the cake. Adding a little more alcohol will bring the colour back to a painting consistency. To save time, you can also use SK Edible Gold and Silver Paint.

Liquid food colours

Liquid food colours can be used for painting on the surface of paste, either neat or diluted further with a few drops of cooled, boiled water or clear alcohol (vodka or gin) to achieve the required strength of colour.

Squires Kitchen produce a wide range of paste, dust and liquid food colours for cake decorating. All Squires Kitchen colours are edible, light-fast, tartrazine-free and glycerine-free.

Creating Texture

Texture is just as important as colour in cake decorating. There are many effects that can be achieved easily just using simple kitchen implements.

A food-grade texture mat or new, plastic pan scourer is suitable to use for creating many textured effects as this cuts into the surface of paste quickly and easily. Press lightly for soft texture, such as fur, and firmly for a deeper texture, such as a grass effect. For grass and fur, you can also use a dinner fork or make lots of tiny cuts in the surface using the tip of a knife.

For a wood effect, press over the surface of rolled out paste with a ruler to create planks and randomly scratch the surface in-between the indented lines with the blade of a knife to resemble wood grain. (Wood-effect embossers are available if you are short of time.)

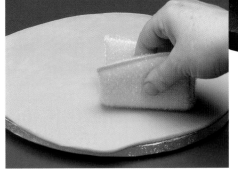

Sticking Items Together

I recommend using an edible glue made from CMC (see recipe on page 11), or you can use a ready-made glue to save time. To secure two items together, brush some edible glue onto the area you are sticking on to (e.g. the neck in preparation for the head, or the shoulder in preparation for the arm) and leave for a few moments to become sticky. Do not use too much or the piece may slide out of place. Press the item onto the glue and twist very slightly backwards and forwards to help hold it firmly in place. Small pieces of food-grade foam sponge can be used to support the piece until dry.

Royal icing can be used as an even stronger glue which, when dry, holds heavier or larger items like the Were-rabbit silhouette (see page 55) firmly in place.

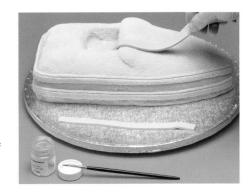

How to Model Wallace and Gromit

Making Wallace

Head

1. To make Wallace's head, first roll a ball of flesh modelling paste into an oval shape and pinch gently at the bottom for the neck. Shape the narrow sides of his head by rolling further between your hands. Push down any excess paste at the top and smooth outwards to make the mouth area fuller. Gently stroke the forehead area up and pinch it forward.

2. Place the head flat on the work surface. Indent the corners of the mouth using a bone or ball tool. Between these two indents, roll the paste gently with the handle of a paintbrush or stroke backwards and forwards with a ball or bone tool to open up the mouth and create a ridge. Don't press in too deeply, especially in the centre, as the teeth will need to be supported there. Run your finger around the corners of the mouth at the top to define the shape.

3. Using a ball or bone tool, indent two eye sockets side by side. Roll a ball-shaped nose and press down to flatten slightly. Stick in place, spaced equally between the eyes and the top of the mouth. For the ears, roll two small balls of paste and indent the centre of each using the ball or bone tool. Cut a tiny piece away from one side to make a straight edge and stick the ears in position on the sides of the head, level with his nose. When you are sticking the ears in place, press gently at the top and bottom and at the outside edge to make them slightly angular.

4. To make the teeth, thinly roll out a little white modelling paste and cut a strip to the required size. Indent along the length of the strip using the back of a knife. When Wallace is smiling and showing all his teeth, cut the bottom set first, usually between seven and nine teeth, and taper the outer teeth slightly. Cut four teeth for the top. After the teeth are inserted, gently stroke along the length of the mouth in a pinching action to close the mouth slightly.

5. Roll two balls of white modelling paste for the eyes and stick on a small, flattened circle of black for the pupil.

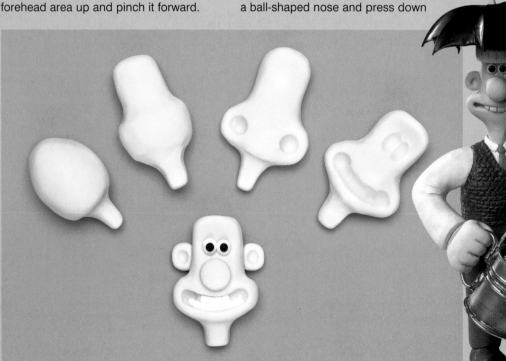

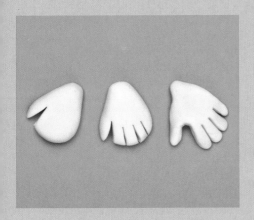

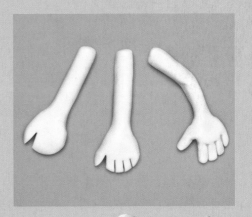

slightly shorter than the thumb cut, and stroke gently to elongate them. Round off the tips by pinching gently. Curve the thumb down towards the palm for a natural position. Pinch at the wrist to round off the hand; the wrist can then be inserted into a sleeve to hold the hand more securely.

Arms

To make an arm, roll some flesh modelling paste into a sausage shape and round off one end. Press the rounded end to flatten it slightly. Follow the instructions above for modelling the hand. Shape the elbow by pushing in gently, and then bend the arm halfway between the wrist and the shoulder and pinch gently at the elbow. Stick in position in the required pose.

Hands

To model a hand, roll a ball of flesh modelling paste into a teardrop shape and press down to flatten slightly. Make a cut for the thumb on one side, cutting halfway between the wrist and the top of the hand. Make three cuts across the top for fingers,

Making Gromit

Head

1. To make Gromit's head, roll a piece of palest brown modelling paste into a ball. Roll the paste gently backwards and forwards between your palms, just above halfway to make a rounded teardrop shape. Roll a paintbrush handle over the eye area to indent the paste and pinch up at the front to shape the forehead. Roll the muzzle between your thumb and finger to elongate and round off. Indent the eye sockets by pressing in with a ball or bone tool.

2. Roll two balls of white modelling paste for the eyes and use small, flattened circles of black for the pupils. Roll a ball of black paste for the nose and

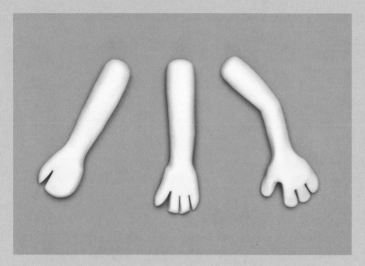

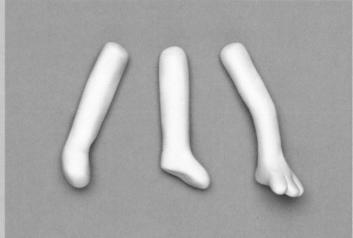

press gently to flatten slightly. Position the nose exactly midway between the eyes and the bottom of his muzzle.

3. For the ears, roll slightly tapered sausages of brown modelling paste and press down on the work surface to flatten slightly. Bend each ear halfway down. Leave to firm for a few moments, and then stick in place, pushing down into the head a little so they are held securely. There is a little space in-between the ears, but for larger modelled figures they are supported better if they are stuck together, or held in place with sugar sticks (see page 13).

Arms

To make an arm, roll a piece of palest brown modelling paste into a sausage and round off one end. Press the rounded end a little to flatten and make a small cut for a thumb on one side, then two cuts across the top for fingers. Pinch gently to round off the tips. Curve the thumb down towards the palm for a natural pose. Shape the elbow by pushing in gently, and then bend the arm halfway between the wrist and the shoulder and pinch gently at the elbow.

Legs

To make a leg, roll some palest brown modelling paste into a sausage and round off one end. Bend the rounded end forward to make a foot and squeeze gently either side at the heel to narrow slightly. Pinch the heel out at the back. Press the bottom of the foot down onto the work surface to flatten and then cut twice to separate the toes, rounding each off by pinching gently.

Body

To make Gromit's body, roll some palest brown modelling paste into a long teardrop shape. At the narrower end, pinch and stroke gently to bring up the neck. Push the neck slightly forward. Stroke the paste down the centre of the body to narrow slightly and smooth to round off the tummy area. To support the head, push a sugar stick down through the neck, leaving a little protruding from the top.

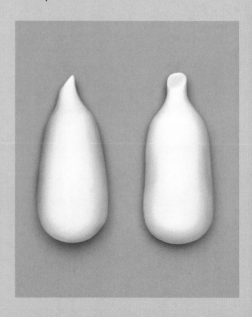

Hints and Tips

Joins

On some of the projects throughout the book I have left joins showing, e.g. the shoulder join on Gromit (see page 35). This is to show that you can still successfully capture the likeness of a character without modelling a perfect replica. For a more accurate likeness, the joins are blended. (Be aware that with some sugarpaste recipes, the joins may not smooth closed as well as others do.)

Wallace's Mouth

For ease of modelling, in most projects throughout the book you will find that Wallace's mouth does not have any shadow added to the hollowed-out smile. If you prefer, the mouth can be filled with a flattened sausage of dark red modelling paste to create shadow (see page 29, Rocket to the Moon) before adding the teeth. Throughout this book, Wallace's mouth is either shown with upper teeth or both upper and lower teeth added. If you are short of time, then a fun 'o' shaped mouth can be indented very quickly using the end of a paintbrush.

Eyes

The eyes on both characters are side-by-side without any space in-between, and are perfect ball shapes with flattened circular pupils. For authenticity, you can indent the centre of each pupil with a cocktail stick if you wish to resemble the beads that are used for the characters' eyes.

Expression

When the forehead on both Wallace and Gromit is moved slightly, it acts as an eyebrow and will significantly change the facial expression. Pushing too far down over the eyes will make an angry or unhappy expression, so be careful not to be heavy-handed unless this is required. Stroking the top part of the face gently upwards and keeping the shape rounded gives the normal expression and is how they are usually depicted. When you want to obtain a questioning or quizzical look, gently push up higher on one side only. As Gromit doesn't have a mouth, the facial expressions you create for him are doubly important.

Colours

To make the flesh colour for Wallace, use a little pink and orange paste colours (or flesh colour if this is available) and knead until thoroughly blended. Use a dark green, such as SK Holly/Ivy, for his jumper and bright red for his tie.

To make the pale brown for Gromit, use a hint of brown paste food colour and use a dark chocolate brown for his ears.

Shortcuts

Gromit's body parts are usually modelled separately, but in some projects where he is wearing his work boots, the body is modelled with the tops of the legs in one piece and his boots are made separately. Instructions for modelling Gromit in this way can be found in the instructions for the relevant projects.

In some instances, where it isn't too noticeable, Gromit's neck has been omitted for ease of modelling. The sugar stick is inserted directly into the top of the body before the head is added directly on top.

Rocket to the Moon

As Wallace once said, "Everybody knows the moon's made of cheese!" so a lunar holiday was planned and Wallace built himself a rocket to take him there. How ingenious!

MATERIALS

2 x 1 litre (2 pint) bowl-shaped sponge cakes

450g (1lb) buttercream

Sugarpaste: 10g ($^1/_4$oz) grey, 1.14kg (2$^1/_2$lb) orange and 550g (1lb 3$^1/_2$oz) pale yellow

Modelling paste: pea-sized ball of black, 2 pea-sized balls of brown, just under 5g ($^1/_4$oz) dark green, tiny ball of dark red, 10g ($^1/_4$oz) flesh, just under 5g ($^1/_4$oz) palest brown, tiny ball of red and 10g ($^1/_4$oz) white

Icing sugar in a sugar shaker

Edible glue

A few drops of cooled, boiled water

1 sugar stick

EQUIPMENT

30cm (12") round cake board

Large and small rolling pins

Pastry brush

Cake smoother

Palette knife

Serrated carving knife

Straight-bladed cutting knife

3cm (1$^1/_4$") and 4.5cm (1$^3/_4$") circle cutters

Ball or bone tool

Plain piping nozzle: no. 3

A few cocktail sticks

Foam pieces (for support)

Recipes and a baking chart can be found on pages 8 to 15

METHOD

Carving the Cakes

1. Trim the crust from each cake and level the tops. Turn the cakes over and trim both cake sides, taking off a ring of cake so each one is more pointed in shape. Cut a layer in each and then sandwich all layers together with buttercream, making the rocket shape, taking care not to overfill each layer. Spread a layer of buttercream over the surface, ensuring that the buttercream completely covers the whole cake.

2. To make the top of the rocket slightly pointed, shape 60g (2oz) of orange sugarpaste into a rounded teardrop, press the rounded end flat and then pinch the paste to create an edge. Stick this piece on top of the rocket, smoothing the join line into the surface. Put the cake aside to allow the surface of the buttercream to firm (this helps when covering the cake later). If the atmosphere is warm, it may help the buttercream surface to firm if the cake is placed in the refrigerator for 10-15 minutes.

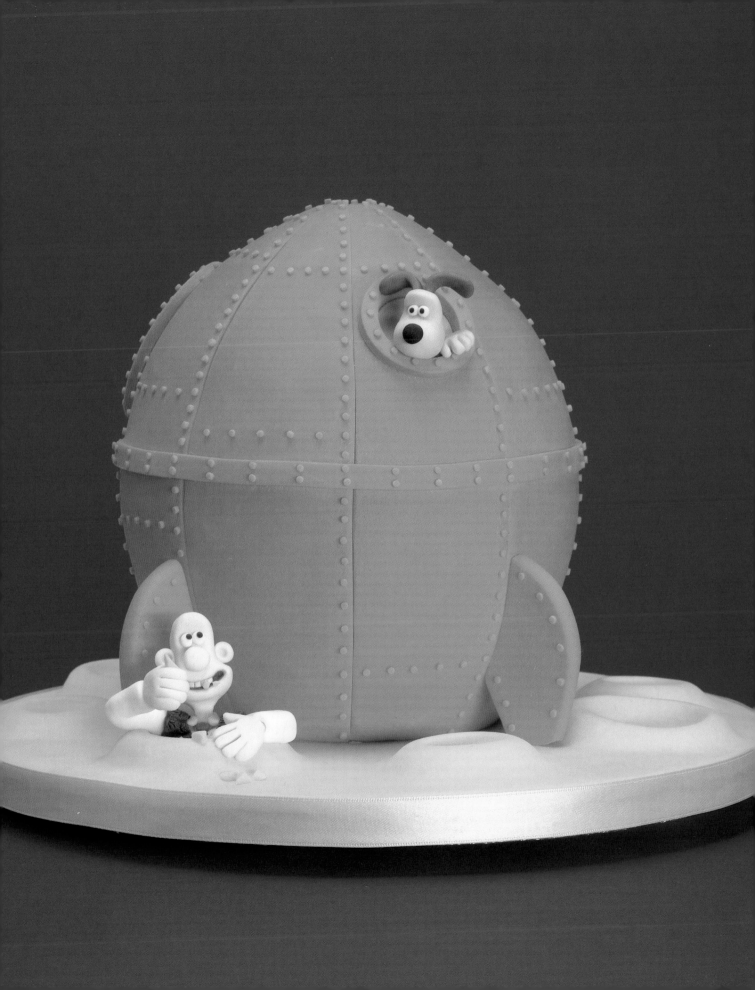

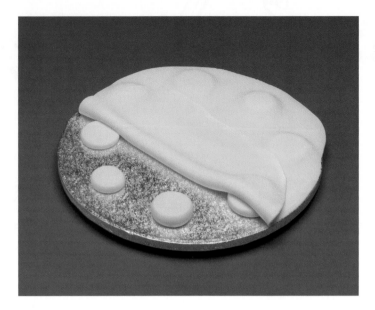

Covering the Cake and Board

3. Knead the pale yellow sugarpaste until soft and pliable. Split 145g (5oz) into eight different sized pieces and shape into flattened circles. Slightly dampen the cake board with a little cooled, boiled water and then stick these circles in place around the edge of the cake board. Roll out the remaining pale yellow sugarpaste on a non-stick board or work surface dusted with a sprinkling of icing sugar to prevent sticking and cover the cake board, smoothing around the shapes to expel any air pockets. Press the end of the large and small rolling pins into each raised circle to make craters. Trim away the excess paste from around the edge and then set aside to dry.

4. When the surface of the buttercream on the cake has set firmly, it is ready to be covered with sugarpaste. Spread a little more buttercream over the surface so the sugarpaste will stick easily or rework the surface with a palette knife that has been dipped in warm, boiled water.

5. Roll out 1kg (2lb 3$^1/_4$oz) of orange sugarpaste and cut a strip measuring the height of the cake and 50cm (20") in length. Sprinkle the surface with icing sugar to prevent sticking and then roll up the strip into a spiral. Place against the cake and unroll the paste around it, then press the join closed and trim off any excess paste. The top will be wide and open, so carefully stretch out any pleats and smooth the excess paste upwards, before trimming it away. Smooth all joins closed and secure with a little edible glue. To remove the joins completely, rub the surface gently with a little icing sugar on your fingers.

6. Use a cake smoother to achieve a smooth surface. Leave to firm up for a few moments, then smooth again. Quickly lift the cake and position it on the cake board. Any marks left from your hands can be smoothed out with a cake smoother whilst the paste is still soft. To mark the sections on the rocket, roll a knife gently over the surface to make a neat indentation. Mark the cake in half first, then into quarters, then mark another line in-between each section so there are eight sections in total.

7. For the porthole window, cut out a circle with the smallest circle cutter and remove the sugarpaste from the centre. Thinly roll out the grey sugarpaste and cut a circle to fill the space. To make the edging, roll out the orange trimmings, cut a hoop using both circle cutters, and stick this in place around the window using edible glue.

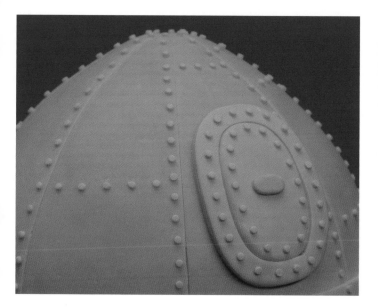

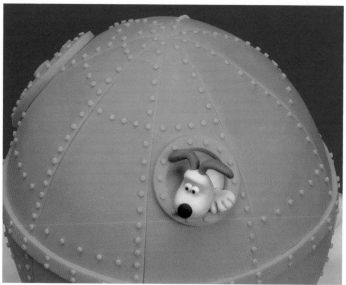

8. To make the door, roll 10g (¹/₄oz) of orange sugarpaste into an oval shape and press the surface flat using a cake smoother. Stick this in position with two sections in-between the door and the porthole window. Roll out a little more paste and cut a strip to edge around the door. Smooth the join closed with your finger. Model a tiny oval-shaped door handle and secure in place.

9. Split 90g (3oz) of orange sugarpaste into quarters to make the rocket supports. Roll each piece into a teardrop shape and press flat with the

cake smoother. Cut off the point and then cut a curve in one side. Stick these in place so that they are spaced evenly around the base of the rocket.

10. Thinly roll out some more orange sugarpaste and put aside for a few moments to allow the surface to firm. Meanwhile, roll out the remaining orange and cut a strip to go around the middle of the cake. Smooth the join to remove it completely.

11. Using the rolled-out orange paste from earlier, cut out all the miniature circles for bolts using the piping

nozzle. Keep pressing repeatedly into the paste, letting all the little circles collect in the nozzle, and then tip them out. To attach the bolts to the surface of the cake easily, first brush a line of edible glue on the cake. Using the brush with only a tiny amount of glue on it, pick up the circles one at a time and position them on the cake.

Tip If you are short of time, instead of cutting individual circles for the bolts, simply indent circles directly onto the surface of the cake using the tip of the piping nozzle.

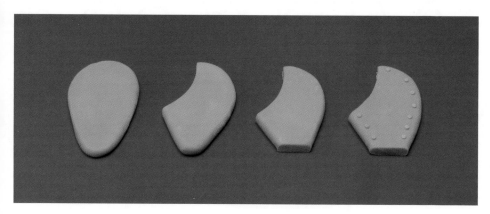

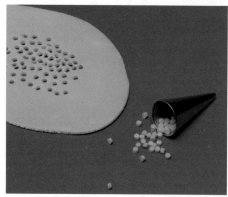

Wallace

12. Model Wallace's two sleeves and chest area first, by rolling 5g (just under $^1/_4$oz) of white modelling paste into a sausage. The shape should be slightly fuller in the centre and measure 8cm (3") in length. Hollow out each end by pressing in with the end of a paintbrush. Bend the paste 1cm ($^3/_8$") from each end to create the elbows and support the pose with foam pieces.

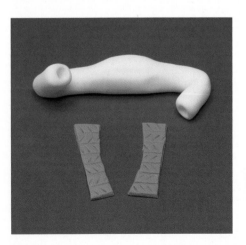

13. For Wallace's pullover, roll out and cut two strips of dark green modelling paste, tapering the centre slightly. Mark lines across each strip and then use a cocktail stick to mark the knit pattern. Stick in position using a little edible glue. For the tie, model a tiny tapered sausage and an even smaller teardrop of red modelling paste, then secure to the pullover. Push a sugar stick down through the centre, leaving a little protruding to support the head.

14. Using 5g (just under $^1/_4$oz) of flesh modelling paste, make Wallace's head following the instructions in the How to Model Wallace and Gromit section (see page 24). Push the head down onto the sugar stick and secure at the base. Thinly roll out a little white modelling paste, cut a small strip for his collar and secure to the neck.

15. Split the remaining flesh modelling paste in half and model Wallace's hands following the instructions in the How to Model Wallace and Gromit section (see page 25). Stick the hands in position and add some of the pale yellow trimmings shaped into crumbs of cheese. Stick some cheese into Wallace's mouth.

Gromit

16. Using the palest brown, brown, white and black modelling paste, make Gromit's head and hand following the instructions in the How to Model Wallace and Gromit section (see pages 25 to 26). Assemble him directly in the porthole window.

"Cracking job, Gromit."

The Great British Sandcastle

Everyone needs a holiday, so the two companions have taken a trip to the seaside. The ingenious Wallace has decided to build a sandcastle in the shape of his slipper, topped off with the Union Jack flag.

MATERIALS

30cm (12") square sponge cake

550g (1lb 3^1/$_2$oz) buttercream

Sugarpaste: 1.5kg (3lb 5oz) golden brown

Modelling paste: 5g (just under ^{1}/$_4$oz) black, 20g (^{3}/$_4$oz) blue, 10g (^{1}/$_4$oz) brown, 10g (^{1}/$_4$oz) dark blue, 160g (5^1/$_2$oz) flesh, 75g (2^1/$_2$oz) palest brown, 175g (6oz) red, 5g (just under ^{1}/$_4$oz) turquoise, 200g (7oz) white and 5g (just under ^{1}/$_4$oz) yellow

Pastillage: 45g (1^1/$_2$oz) golden brown

Icing sugar in a sugar shaker

Edible glue

A few drops of cooled, boiled water

2 sugar sticks

5ml (1tsp) brown sugar

EQUIPMENT

35cm (14") oval-shaped cake board

Large and small rolling pins

Pastry brush

Cake smoother

Palette knife

Serrated carving knife

Straight-bladed cutting knife

Sable paintbrush: no. 2 (SK)

0.5cm (^{1}/$_8$"), 2cm (^{3}/$_4$") and 5cm (2") circle cutters

Bone or ball tool

New, clean pan scourer

A few cocktail sticks

Recipes and a baking chart can be found on pages 8 to 15

METHOD

Preparation

1. To allow for drying time, make the pastillage windbreak stakes, flagpole, spade pole and handle first. For the stakes, roll out the pastillage and cut three strips measuring 18cm (7") in length. Roll a small sausage for the flagpole measuring 5cm (2") in length. For the spade, roll a thick sausage measuring 6cm (2^1/$_2$") long and taper slightly at both ends. Roll another smaller one for the handle at the top.

2. Thinly roll out 5g (just under ^{1}/$_4$oz) of white modelling paste and cut a rectangle for the flag. Stick in place with one end wrapped around the flagpole. Thinly roll out a little red and dark blue modelling paste cut out red strips and dark blue triangular shapes to make the flag pattern. Stick in place with edible glue and then set the flag aside to dry.

3. Trim the crust from the cake and slice the top flat. Cut the cake exactly in half and stack one piece on top of the other. Trim either side at the front to

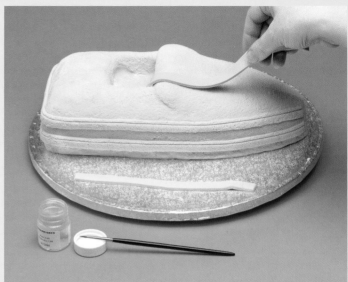

narrow the toe area. Trim along the top edge to round off and trim the corners from the back. Just beyond halfway, cut out the seat area measuring 9cm (3^1/$_2$") square, cutting down to the first layer of cake.

4. Spread buttercream on the underside of the cake and position on the cake board. Sandwich the layers together and then spread a layer of buttercream over the surface of the cake to help the sugarpaste stick.

5. Roll a 30g (1oz) sausage of golden brown sugarpaste, press down to flatten and use to build up the flap on top of the slipper. Using a sprinkling of icing sugar to prevent sticking, roll out 650g (1lb 7oz) of golden brown sugarpaste on a non-stick board or work surface. Press over the surface of the paste with the scourer to texture. Lift the paste and cover the cake, stretching out any pleats and smoothing down and around the shape, pushing gently

into the seat. Trim away the excess from around the base and texture further using the scourer.

6. Cut strips of golden brown sugarpaste and position them in a weaved, tartan-effect pattern. Texture each strip as you attach it and mark a neat line along each one using the back of a knife. Stick on a small, flattened circle at the toe area and texture as before. Model the small sandcastle for the flag, texture as before and stick on top of the toe area.

7. Dampen the cake board around the cake with a little cooled, boiled water. Unevenly roll out the remaining golden brown sugarpaste and press in place around the cake board. Push the paste up against the

sandcastle and texture the surface. Press firmly with the scourer to blend the joins and trim away any excess paste from around the base. Build up three mounds at the back and texture as before. These will be used for the windbreak stakes later.

Wallace

8. To make Wallace's rubber ring, roll 75g (2^1/$_2$oz) of white modelling paste into a ball and press down on the surface with a cake smoother until the circle is 8cm (3") in diameter. Cut out a 5cm (2") circle from the centre using the circle cutter. Make another ring in the same way using red modelling paste and stick one on top of the other, smoothing around the edge to close the join. Mark pleats with a cocktail stick.

9. For Wallace's legs, split 35g (1^1/$_4$oz) of flesh modelling paste in half and roll two sausages measuring 6cm (2^1/$_2$") in length. Stick them together with a little edible glue.

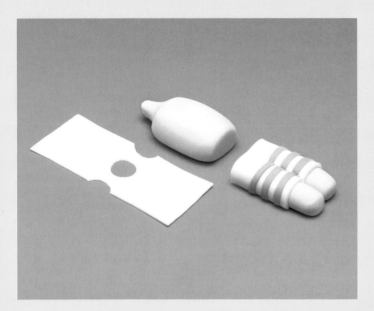

For the shorts, thinly roll out 5g (¹/₄oz) of white modelling paste and cut a strip to cover the top of the legs. Push in-between the legs using the back of a knife. Thinly roll out some blue modelling paste, cut several stripes and secure these to the shorts using edible glue.

10. For Wallace's body, roll 60g (2oz) of flesh modelling paste into an oval shape and pinch at the top for the neck. Thinly roll out some white modelling paste and cut a strip the width of Wallace's body and long enough to cover the front and back. Cut a small circle for the neck hole in the centre of the strip using the 2cm (³/₄") circle cutter then cut either side for armholes. Stick this strip in position on his body, smoothing the join closed down either side. Check that the body fits inside the rubber ring, adjust if necessary and then remove.

11. Thinly roll out some blue modelling paste and cut stripes as before. Stick the legs into the opening. Push the body into the rubber ring and then stick this on top of the legs. Make sure you have left enough room for Gromit.

12. Make the flask next by rolling 10g (¹/₄oz) of blue modelling paste into a sausage and cutting the top and bottom straight. Stick on a large flattened circle at the base and a smaller circle on the top. Model a red cup for the top and add a little loop for the handle.

13. Make Wallace's arms using 45g (1¹/₂oz) of flesh modelling paste split in half, following the instructions in the How to Model Wallace and Gromit section (see page 25). Stick each arm in position with one hand holding the flask and the other resting on the back of the slipper.

Gromit

14. To make Gromit's book, thickly roll out 5g (just under ¹/₄oz) of white modelling paste, cut an oblong and mark down the centre using the flat of a knife. Mark lines around the outside edge for pages. For the cover, roll out some brown modelling paste, stick the pages down onto it with edible glue and cut around the shape, leaving an edge.

Pinch the book to close it slightly and then set aside.

15. For Gromit's body, roll a 30g (1oz) oval of palest brown modelling paste and narrow the top. Push the body into the sandcastle next to Wallace. Insert a sugar stick down into the body until a little is protruding to help hold his head secure later. Split 10g (¹/₄oz) of palest brown paste in half, roll two sausages for his legs, bend each one and stick against his body in the sandcastle.

16. For Gromit's arms, split 15g (¹/₂oz) of palest brown modelling paste in half and follow the instructions given in the How to Model Wallace and Gromit section (see page 26). Stick his arms in position holding the book.

17. Using the remaining palest brown modelling paste, make Gromit's head following the modelling instructions (see pages 25-26). You will not need to make the eyes as he is wearing sunglasses. Use the remaining flesh modelling paste to make Wallace's head, following the modelling instructions (see page 24). Do not make the neck as this was included with the body.

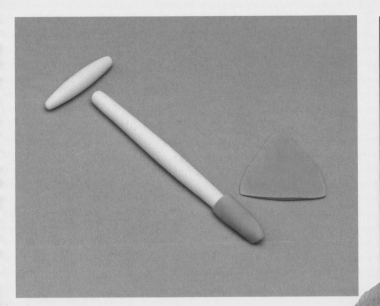

18. To make Gromit's sunglasses, roll two little sausages of yellow modelling paste and round off one end. Press the rounded ends flat and cut out the centre using the 0.5cm ($^1/_8$") circle cutter. Stretch the paste to elongate the cut out shape and stick in position over Gromit's eyes. Thinly roll out a small piece of blue modelling paste and cut out two circles to fill the spaces, stretching the shape to fit.

To Finish

19. To make the turquoise spade, first cover the end of the pastillage pole with a small piece of turquoise modelling paste. Model a small teardrop and roll flat, cut the top straight and stick in place wrapped around the back. Stick in position with the handle resting against the sandcastle. For the red spade, shape a small oblong for the top and cut out the centre using the 0.5cm ($^1/_8$") circle cutter. Roll a small ball, press in the centre with your finger and then cut off one side. Stick this piece into the sand. Roll a sausage of red paste and stick this on top with the handle, again resting it against the sandcastle for support.

20. For the bucket, roll the remaining dark blue modelling paste into a teardrop and pinch into the full end to indent the paste. Smooth around the rim and press down on the point to flatten the base. Half-bury the bucket and fill with golden brown textured trimmings for sand. For the handle, roll a yellow sausage, rounding off both ends and stick in place looped round the bucket.

21. Shape the remaining white modelling paste into flattened teardrop shapes for the shells and indent radiating lines by pressing over the surface with a cocktail stick.

22. Sprinkle the brown sugar over the cake and cake board. When dry, push the flag into the small sandcastle.

23. Push the windbreak stakes down into the mounds of sand at the back of the cake. Using white and red modelling paste, cut out strips and indent along the surface slightly by smoothing with your fingers. Make the first one (white) a little thicker to help support the next. Attach the strips to the stakes, one on top of the other.

"Oh this is absolutely **FANTASTIC."**

Wallace

This Wallace cake is quick and easy to achieve and is perfect if you are short of time or if you are a novice cake decorator. You can present the cake as it is, or make Gromit (see pages 41 to 43) and put them side by side on the party table for a stunning centrepiece.

MATERIALS

23cm (9") round sponge cake

450g (1lb) buttercream

Sugarpaste: small piece of black, 400g (14oz) dark green, 15g (^{1}/$_2$oz) dark red, 1kg (2lb 3^1/$_4$oz) flesh and 75g (2^1/$_2$oz) white

Icing sugar in a sugar shaker

Edible glue

A few drops of cooled, boiled water

EQUIPMENT

30cm (12") round cake board

Large rolling pin

Pastry brush

Cake smoother

Palette knife

Serrated carving knife

Straight-bladed cutting knife

Sable paintbrush: no. 2 (SK)

1.5cm (^{1}/$_2$") square cutter

Template (see page 120)

Recipes and a baking chart can be found on pages 8 to 15

METHOD

Covering the Board

1. Knead the dark green sugarpaste until soft and pliable. Roll out on a non-stick board or work surface dusted with a sprinkling of icing sugar to prevent sticking and cover the cake board. Trim away any excess paste from around the edge and smooth the surface with a cake smoother. Set aside to dry.

Carving and Covering the Cake

2. Trim the crust from the cake and slice the top flat. Cut out Wallace's head shape using the template, and then cut two even layers in the cake. Cut out Wallace's mouth using the template, cutting down to the first layer. Trim around the top edge of the cake to round off.

3. Spread the base of the cake with buttercream and position on the cake board. Sandwich all layers together with buttercream and then spread a layer over the surface of the cake to help the sugarpaste stick.

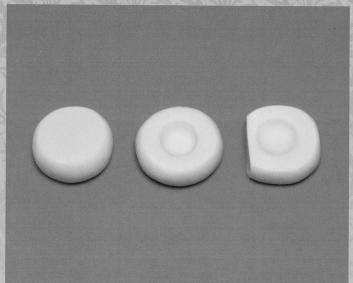

4. Roll out 675g (1lb 7³/₄oz) of flesh coloured sugarpaste and cover the cake completely, stretching out any pleats and smoothing the paste downwards and around the shape. Neatly trim away the excess from around the base, cutting inwards slightly to curve round the edge. To define the inside of the mouth, smooth an edge with your fingertip. Push the end of a rolling pin into the eye area to indent sockets and then smooth the indentation with your fingers.

5. Thinly roll out the dark red sugarpaste and cut the mouth shape slightly smaller than the template. Position inside the mouth and then secure with a dab of edible glue. Thinly roll out 20g (³/₄oz) of white sugarpaste and cut squares for teeth using the square cutter. Press down on each square to soften the cut edge and then stick in position in the mouth, trimming the teeth at the corners of the mouth so they fit neatly.

6. For Wallace's nose, roll 125g (4¹/₂oz) of flesh into a ball and press down on the work surface to flatten slightly. Stick in place on the centre of his face. For the ears, split 145g (5oz) of flesh paste in half and shape into two flattened circles. Indent the centre of each with the end of the rolling pin, smoothing the indentation with your fingers as before. Cut a straight edge on each ear and stick in place with a little edible glue. Smooth the outside edge of both ears to make them slightly angular.

7. For Wallace's neck, roll the remaining flesh sugarpaste into a teardrop shape and press down to flatten slightly. Cut the top and bottom straight and stick in position. To make the eyes, split the remaining white sugarpaste in half and roll into ball shapes. Stick in position with a flattened black circle on each for the pupils.

"Please Wallace, call me Totty."

Gromit

This sculpted Gromit cake is perfect if you are a beginner or short of time as it can be easily decorated in under an hour. If you need more servings, team it together with Wallace (see pages 38 to 40) and present them side by side.

(see pages 38 to 40)

MATERIALS

5cm x 15cm (10" x 6") oblong sponge cake

1 litre (2 pint) bowl-shaped sponge cake

450g (1lb) buttercream

Sugarpaste: 175g (6oz) black, 1kg (2lb 3¼oz) palest brown, 400g (14oz) red and 60g (2oz) white

Icing sugar in a sugar shaker

Edible glue

A few drops of cooled, boiled water

EQUIPMENT

30cm (12") round cake board

Large rolling pin

Pastry brush

Cake smoother

Palette knife

Serrated carving knife

Straight-bladed cutting knife

Sable paintbrush: no. 2 (SK)

Template (see page 121)

Recipes and a baking chart can be found on pages 8 to 15

METHOD

Covering the Board

1. Knead the red sugarpaste until soft and pliable, roll out on a non-stick board or work surface dusted with a sprinkling of icing sugar to prevent sticking and cover the cake board. Trim away any excess paste from around the edge and smooth the surface with a cake smoother. Set aside to dry.

Carving and Covering the Cake

2. Trim the crust from each cake and slice the tops flat. Cut out Gromit's head shape from the oblong cake using the template. Place the bowl-shaped cake in position for the muzzle and then trim around the cake to remove any ridges and to round off the top edge. Use some of the cake trimmings to build up Gromit's forehead.

3. Spread buttercream on the underside of the cake and position centrally on the cake board. Sandwich the layers together and then spread buttercream over the surface of the cake to help the sugarpaste stick.

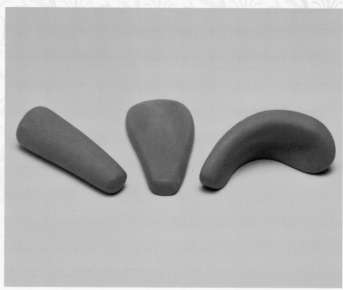

4. Roll out the palest brown sugarpaste and cover the cake completely, stretching out any pleats and smoothing downwards and around the shape. Trim away the excess paste from around the base and tuck the edges underneath the cake to round off the base slightly. Push the end of the rolling pin into the eye area to indent sockets side by side, and then rub gently with your fingers to soften the indentation. Rub over the surface with a cake smoother.

5. Split the white sugarpaste in half, roll into ball-shaped eyes and stick in place with a little edible glue. Stick on two flattened circles of black sugarpaste for the pupils. For his nose, roll the remaining black sugarpaste into a ball, press down to flatten slightly and then stick centrally onto Gromit's muzzle.

6. For the ears, split the brown sugarpaste in half and roll into long teardrop shapes. Press each one down to flatten slightly, bend halfway and then stick onto the cake board with the narrow end attached to the top of Gromit's head, leaving a little space in-between.

"Honestly lad. I don't know what's got into you lately."

Crackers about Cheese!

Hutch is the cute, though ever-hungry, little bunny used in Wallace's fateful experiment to cure the rabbits' vegetable ravaging behaviour. But now, worryingly, he's turned to Wallace's favourite food – cheese.

MATERIALS

20cm (8") round sponge cake

450g (1lb) buttercream

Sugarpaste: 370g (13oz) pale brown, 60g (2oz) pale red and 900g (2lb) pale yellow

Modelling paste: tiny ball of black, 10g ($^1/_4$oz) dark red, 45g (1$^1/_2$oz) green, 60g (2oz) mid-brown, 30g (1oz) pale brown, just under 5g ($^1/_8$oz) palest pink and just under 5g ($^1/_8$oz) white

Paste food colours: green and red (SK)

Dust food colour: white (SK) (optional)

Icing sugar in a sugar shaker

Edible glue

A few drops of cooled, boiled water

EQUIPMENT

25cm (10") square cake board

Large and small rolling pins

Pastry brush

Cake smoother

Palette knife

Serrated carving knife

Straight-bladed cutting knife

Sable paintbrushes: nos. 1, 2 and 6 (SK)

Paint palette

1cm ($^3/_8$") and 10cm (4") circle cutters

New, clean pan scourer

A few cocktail sticks

Ruler

Foam pieces (for support)

Recipes and a baking chart can be found on pages 8 to 15

METHOD

Covering the Board

1. Knead the pale brown sugarpaste until soft and pliable. Slightly dampen the cake board with a little cooled, boiled water, roll out the sugarpaste on a non-stick board or work surface dusted with a sprinkling of icing sugar to prevent sticking and cover the cake board. Smooth the surface with a cake smoother and trim away the excess paste from around the edge. To indent the lines, mark every 5cm (2") along opposite sides of the cake board, line up the ruler against the marks and press down firmly, moving the ruler backwards and forwards slightly. Mark lines to resemble wood grain using a knife and then set aside to dry.

Carving and Covering the Cakes

2. Cut the cake exactly in half and set one half aside. From the remaining half, cut a triangular shaped wedge measuring 6cm (2$^1/_2$") across at the outside edge and a 10cm (4") circle. Cut one third off the depth of this circle to make two circular cakes. Shape both of these to round off the top and bottom edges. Cut a small

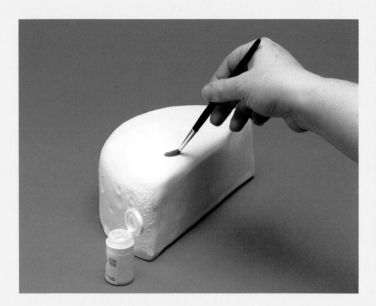

wedge out of the smaller circular cake. Cut two layers in the half that was set aside earlier and sandwich back together with buttercream. Cut one layer in the larger round cake and sandwich back together. Spread a layer of buttercream over the surface of all the cakes to help the sugarpaste stick.

3. Roll out 595g (1lb 5oz) of pale yellow sugarpaste and cover the large cake completely, stretching out any pleats and smoothing the paste downwards. If the pleats are stubborn at the corners, slice away the excess paste and press the join closed, sticking with a little edible glue if necessary. Smooth the join with a little icing sugar on your fingers to remove the mark completely. Trim away any excess paste from around the base and press the front with a cake smoother to remove any marks.

4. To achieve a pitted cheese crust effect, texture the top and back of the cake by pressing a scourer over the surface and indent markings using the end of a paintbrush and your fingers. Brush some white dust food colour over the surface, or alternatively use a

sprinkling of icing sugar. Spread buttercream on the underside of the cake and position on the cake board.

5. Roll out 145g (5oz) of pale yellow sugarpaste and cover the triangular-shaped wedge, smoothing down and around the shape. Pull away the excess paste at the narrow end and cut away in a slice, pinching the join closed. Mark the holes by pressing the end of a paintbrush and the rolling pin into the surface. Position this piece on top of the large cheese, close to the edge so it will support Hutch later, and use a little buttercream to secure it in place.

6. Roll out 145g (5oz) of pale yellow sugarpaste and cover the large round cake next, smoothing down and around the shape and trimming the excess paste from around the base. Spread buttercream on the underside of the cake and position on the cake board. Press the top only with a cake smoother to flatten.

7. Roll out 10g (¹/₄oz) of pale yellow sugarpaste and cover the cut area on the smaller circular cake. Thinly roll out the pale red sugarpaste and cover the

remaining part, trimming a neat line to edge the yellow. Trim around the base and tuck any excess paste underneath. Spread a little buttercream on the underside and stick in position on the cake board.

8. Shape the pale yellow trimmings into flattened circles for the smaller cheeses and indent holes into the surface of one. For the teeth marks on the other, cut a small curve out and then make circular cuts in the surface using the small circle cutter. Thinly roll out some dark red modelling paste and cover the top and sides, sticking the paste with a little edible glue. Cut wedges and crumbs from the pale yellow trimmings and set aside.

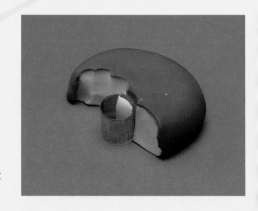

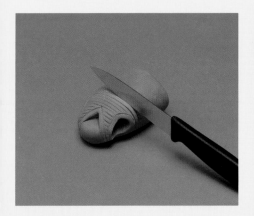

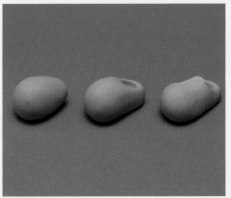

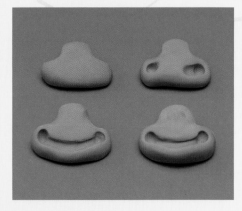

Hutch

9. To make the pullover, shape the green modelling paste into a rounded teardrop. Push into the full end and pinch an edge. Indent the neck area by pressing in with the tip of a knife. Push a ball or bone tool into either side to indent armholes. For the knitted texture, roll the knife over the surface to mark lines and then mark the pattern using the tip of a cocktail stick. Stick the pullover onto the cake, securing with a little edible glue, and push up at the front slightly to make room for the legs.

10. Split just under 5g (¹/₈oz) of mid-brown modelling paste into three pieces. Roll two of these pieces into sausages measuring 2cm (³/₄") in length for the legs. Stick in position against the base of the pullover. Shape the third piece into a teardrop shape, press flat and stick into the neck area.

11. For the slippers, split 25g (just over ³/₄oz) of pale brown modelling paste in half and roll into rounded teardrop shapes. Push into the narrow end using the end of a paintbrush to indent a hole and wind the paintbrush round to open up the hole further. Pinch the front of the indentation forward for the flap and stroke across the top of each slipper to indent and round off the toe area.

12. Dilute a little green and red paste food colours separately with a few drops of cooled, boiled water to achieve a paint consistency. Using the fine paintbrush, paint a checked pattern over the slippers. Paint the green lines first, leave to dry and then paint the red.

13. When the painted surface is dry, split the remaining pale brown modelling paste in half for the soles. Roll into sausages, indent just below half way and then press these flat, stroking each toe area to widen. Stick the soles onto the slippers and indent the heel by pressing in with the flat of a knife. Stick in position on the cake and support with foam pieces if necessary.

14. For Hutch's arms, split 10g (¹/₄oz) of mid-brown modelling paste in half and follow the instructions for making Wallace's arms in the How to Model Wallace and Gromit section (see page 25). Stick in position with a small piece of cheese in his hand, using a piece of foam sponge to support the arm until dry.

15. To make Hutch's head, shape 45g (1¹/₂oz) of mid-brown modelling paste into a flattened circle and pinch either side at the top to narrow the eye area. Push the ball or bone tool into the corners of the mouth and then indent to open up the smile. Indent two eye sockets side by side.

16. Thinly roll out some white modelling paste and cut a strip for the bottom teeth. Indent eight times along the length to mark nine teeth, trim to narrow slightly at either end, and then stick in place. Roll a pea-sized piece of white modelling paste into a short sausage and press flat. Cut in half and use for the two front teeth. Roll two balls for eyes, secure in place and stick on tiny flattened circles of black paste for pupils. Shape one third of the palest pink modelling paste into an oval for his nose and indent nostrils using a cocktail stick.

17. Split the remaining mid-brown modelling paste in half and use this to make the ears. Roll each piece into a long teardrop shape and indent the centre with the handle of a paintbrush. Fill the indentation a with teardrop shapes of palest pink paste and smooth down with your fingertips. Stick the ears in place and curve them round, ensuring they are supported by the wedge of cheese. Stick some crumbs into Hutch's mouth and sprinkle the remainder around the cake.

"Cheeeeeeese!"

Anti-pesto Van

Wallace and Gromit have ventured out in their Anti-pesto van with their trusty rabbit catching equipment!

MATERIALS

28cm (11") square sponge cake
450g (1lb) buttercream
Sugarpaste: 90g (3oz) black, 600g (1lb 5^1/$_4$oz) green, 820g (1lb 13oz) pale blue/green
Modelling paste: 115g (4oz) black, 85g (2^3/$_4$oz) blue, 5g (just under ^{1}/$_4$oz) cream, just under 5g (^{1}/$_8$oz) dark brown, 15g (^{1}/$_2$oz) flesh, 15g (^{1}/$_2$oz) grey, 15g (^{1}/$_2$oz) mid-brown, 5g (^{1}/$_8$oz) orange, 5g (^{1}/$_8$oz) pale pink, 45g (1^1/$_2$oz) palest brown, 5g (just under ^{1}/$_4$oz) white and a tiny ball of yellow
Pastillage: 10g (^{1}/$_4$oz) cream
Paste food colours: black, brown and white (SK)
Metallic lustre dust food colour: bronze and silver (SK)
Icing sugar in a sugar shaker
Edible glue
A few drops of cooled, boiled water
15ml (1tbsp) clear alcohol (e.g. vodka or gin)
4 sugar sticks

EQUIPMENT

30cm (12") round cake board
Large and small rolling pins
Pastry brush
Palette knife
Serrated carving knife
Straight-bladed cutting knife
Sable paintbrushes: nos. 1 and 2 (SK)
0.7cm (^{3}/$_8$"), 1.5cm (^{1}/$_2$") and 2.5cm (1") circle cutters
1.5cm (^{1}/$_2$") square cutter
New, clean pan scourer
Clingfilm (plastic food wrap)
Plain piping nozzle: no. 3
A few cocktail sticks
Foam pieces (for support)
Templates (see page 122)

Recipes and a baking chart can be found on pages 8 to 15

METHOD

Carving and Covering the Cake

1. Trim the crust from the cake and slice the top flat. Cut the cake exactly in half. Cut a layer in each half and then stack all layers one on top of each other. To shape the van's front windscreen, measure 10cm (4") from the front of the cake and cut down at a slight outward angle towards the front, cutting down to a depth of 3cm (1^1/$_4$"). From this cut, slice away a wedge to the front of the cake. Round off the front of the van for the bonnet, keeping height either side for wings.

2. Shape the back of the van to slope down and outwards to the base. Trim the sides of the cake from the top for the windows either side of the van, cutting down and outwards level with the base of the windscreen, leaving a slight ridge. Trim down either side of the cake from this ridge to round off. Sandwich all layers together with buttercream and then spread a layer over the surface of the cake to help the sugarpaste stick. Spread buttercream on the underside of the cake and then position on

the cake board, leaving space on one side for the modelled figures.

3. Thinly roll out the black sugarpaste using a sprinkling of icing sugar to prevent sticking and cut a long strip 2.5cm (1") deep to go around the base of the cake. Sprinkle a little more icing sugar over the surface of this strip and then roll up into a spiral (this will make it easier to pick up). Position the strip against the base of the cake and unroll it around around the cake. Trim off the excess paste from the join and smooth it closed.

4. Roll out 800g (1lb 12oz) of pale blue/green sugarpaste and cover the cake, smoothing the paste around the shape and trimming a neat line 1.5cm (1/2") from the base. This covering needs detailing on the surface so cover areas you are not working on with clingfilm to keep the paste soft. First, trim four curves to make space for the tyres and then smooth all the ridges and indentations using your

fingers dusted with a little icing sugar. This may cause the covering to be pushed down and make the base uneven, so re-trim if necessary.

5. Using a straight-bladed knife, mark a line around the top of the van. Using the templates, mark all the windows and detailing around them. When marking lines, gently roll the knife into the surface to prevent pulling and tearing. For the wound down window, cut out half of the window and remove the top piece of sugarpaste. Thinly roll out a little black sugarpaste and fill this area.

6. The front bumper is extended slightly, so to support this, roll 5g (just under 1/4oz) of blue/green sugarpaste trimmings into a sausage measuring the width of the van. Stick this in place using edible glue and

smooth the top flat. Thinly roll out some more blue/green sugarpaste and cut out the bonnet shape using the template. Smooth around the edge and then stick the bonnet centrally in place. Split 15g (1/2oz) of paste in half and roll sausage-shaped bumpers for the front and back, indenting little circles for bolts on the front bumper only using a no. 3 plain piping nozzle.

7. To make the grille, model a teardrop using 5g (just under 1/4oz) of blue/green sugarpaste and press flat. Cut the bottom straight, mark detailing with the back of a knife and use a cocktail stick for the little holes at the top. Model a tiny sausage from the trimmings and stick this onto the top of the line down the centre.

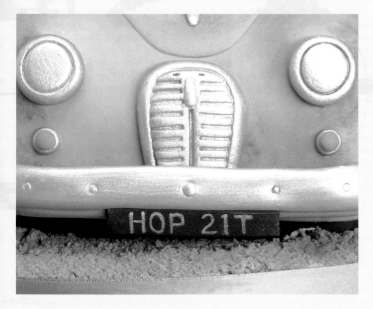

8. Use the remaining blue/green sugarpaste for the detailing on the van. Cut out a small square for the top of the van, two circles for the base of the warning light on the top of the van, shape small, flattened circles for the petrol cap and back light bases, and model three long teardrop-shaped door handles for the sides and for the back.

9. Shape the wing mirrors from 1cm ($^3/_8$") circles and indent the centre to cup them slightly. Model two flattened circles for the headlights, indenting the centre of each using the 1.5cm ($^1/_2$") circle cutter. Roll two tiny sausages of paste for the windscreen wipers. Make the emblem for the bonnet and cut a small hole from the centre using the piping nozzle. Make and attach two flattened circles for the indicators (the lights will be added later).

10. For the wheels, split 75g (2$^1/_2$oz) of black modelling paste into four equally sized pieces. Roll each piece into a ball and press to flatten slightly. Mark the centre using the largest circle cutter then press into the centre to indent. Stick the wheels in place on the van. Split just

under 5g ($^1/_8$oz) of black modelling paste into four and shape four balls for the centre of each wheel. Roll out some more black modelling paste, cut out two black license plates and set aside to dry.

Grass

11. Brush the cake board around the cake with cooled, boiled water. Roll out the green sugarpaste a little at a time and press the scourer firmly into the surface to create a grass effect. Stick the pieces in place over the cake board and around the van, pressing the joins closed by texturing further.

Finishing the Van

12. Mix a little silver metallic lustre dust food colour with the clear alcohol to create a smooth paint. Stipple a little silver paint over the windscreen and

windows for a glass effect. Paint all the silver detailing on the van with a thin coat, allow to dry and then repeat until a smooth covering is achieved. Using a fine paintbrush, paint the wording 'HOP 2IT' on each license plate, allow to dry and then stick in place.

13. Dilute a little black paste food colour with clear alcohol and paint the edging around the windscreen and each window. Dilute the colouring a little further and then stipple a little over the windscreen and windows to create shadows. Add a little brown paste food colour to the diluted black and stipple a tiny amount around the van, especially around the bumpers, hinges and lights.

14. Use the orange modelling paste to make little flattened circles for all the lights and an oval shaped warning light for the top of the van. Using the template, paint the lettering on the side of the van using diluted white paste food colour and a fine paintbrush.

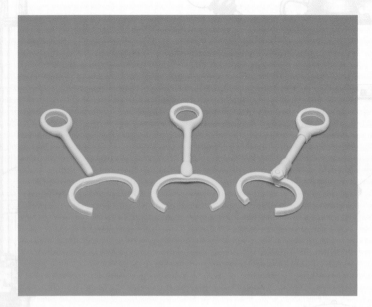

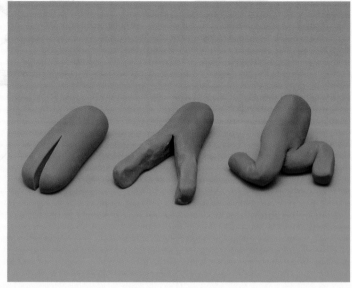

Rabbit Catcher

15. To make the rabbit catcher, roll half of the cream coloured pastillage into a sausage shape and round off one end. Press the rounded end flat and then cut out a circle from the centre using the 1.5cm ($\frac{1}{2}$") circle cutter. Roll out the remaining piece of pastillage. Cut out a 2.5cm (1") circle from the centre, then cut another circle to make a hoop. Cut into this hoop, open and then set aside to dry.

16. To assemble the two parts together, flatten two pea-sized oval shapes and stick in place, one on the top of the join and the other underneath. To hold these pieces securely, thinly roll out some pastillage, cut a strip and wrap it around the two pieces with the join on the underside. Cut another thinner strip for the bottom of the handle. For the bolt nut, shape a tiny flattened circle and indent into the centre with a piping nozzle. Make angular cuts around the outside edge and stick in place. Paint the rabbit catcher using the black, silver and bronze food colours diluted with clear alcohol.

Wallace and Gromit

17. To make Wallace's outfit, roll a sausage using 65g (2$\frac{1}{4}$oz) of blue modelling paste and make a cut halfway up the length to separate the legs. Pinch down both sides to remove the ridges. Bend the legs into a kneeling position, pinch at the knees and mark fabric effect pleats with a cocktail stick. Support the pose using a small piece of foam. Push a sugar stick down through the top until only a little is protruding to help hold the head in place. Set aside to dry.

18. For the boots, split 5g (just under $\frac{1}{4}$oz) of black modelling paste in half and roll each piece into a sausage shape, bending halfway. Pinch out heels at the back and flatten the top. Make another pair of boots for Gromit and set aside.

19. Break 5g (just under $\frac{1}{4}$oz) of black modelling paste into crumbs and scatter in a circle for a rabbit hole, sticking the pieces in place with edible glue. Using the grey, brown, cream, pale pink and a little white, black and yellow modelling paste, make all the bunnies and the daisy following modelling instructions on pages 106 to 107.

20. To make Gromit's body and legs, roll 30g (1oz) of palest brown modelling paste into a sausage shape and make a small cut to separate the legs. Smooth front and back to remove the ridges and cut the legs straight at the bottom so the boots fit neatly. Smooth the top of the body upwards to narrow slightly and push a sugar stick down through the top as before. Place down flat to dry.

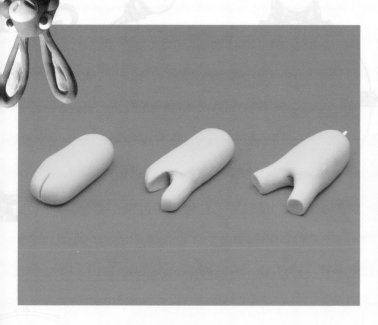

21. Make Wallace and Gromit's heads next, following the modelling instructions (see pages 24-26). Use 10g ($^1/_4$oz) of flesh modelling paste for Wallace and 10g ($^1/_4$oz) of palest brown for Gromit. When modelled, slice off the top of each head so the caps will sit neatly. Make a small hole in Wallace's neck and at the bottom of Gromit's head ready for the sugar stick and then set aside to dry.

22. Make Gromit's arms (see page 26) using 5g (just under $^1/_4$oz) of palest brown modelling paste split in half. For Wallace's sleeves, split 10g ($^1/_4$oz) of blue modelling paste in half and roll two sausages, hollowing out the end of each slightly. Stick in place on both figures, smoothing the join closed as before. Mark fabric effect creases using a cocktail stick.

23. For Wallace's hands, use 5g (just under $^1/_4$oz) split in half and follow the instructions for modelling (see page 25). Mould the hands into their pose, holding onto the rabbit catcher, sticking each wrist securely into

the sleeves. Stick the boots in position, using a strip of mid-brown modelling paste to hold them in place.

24. Use the blue modelling paste trimmings to make the detailing on Wallace's outfit. Thinly roll out and cut a strip for the belt, yoke and pocket. Cut out tiny buttons using the piping nozzle. Paint these buttons with diluted silver lustre food dust and paint a small buckle on the front of the belt. Push the head down onto the sugar stick and stick at the base with a little edible glue. Thinly roll out some blue modelling paste and cut a strip for the collar.

25. Assemble Gromit and stick him securely against the van door. To make the caps, split 5g (just under $^1/_4$oz) of blue modelling paste in half. Roll one half into a ball, cut in half and mark a cross in the top of each using a knife. Split the remaining

piece in half and model two flattened oval shapes for each cap peak. Assemble each cap in place and smooth each peak up at the front.

"An hour, I can't wait an hour! I have a major infestation!"

Rabbit Hunt

A familiar image from 'The Curse of the Were-rabbit', the Anti-pesto team are trying to capture the enormous and terrifying vegetable munching Were-rabbit, in the dead of night...

MATERIALS

20cm (8") square sponge cake
450g (1lb) buttercream
Sugarpaste: 1.14kg (2lb 8oz) mid-blue
Modelling paste: 15g ($^1/_2$oz) black, 45g
(1$^1/_2$oz) blue/grey, just under 5g ($^1/_4$oz)
brown, just under 15g ($^1/_2$oz) flesh, 10g
($^1/_4$oz) green, 20g ($^3/_4$oz) grey/brown, 5g
(just under $^1/_4$oz) mid-brown, 30g (1oz)
orange and 30g (1oz) palest brown
Pastillage: just under 5g ($^1/_8$oz) brown, 225g
(8oz) dark grey and 30g (1oz) pale yellow
Royal icing: 30g (1oz) white
Paste food colour: brown (SK)
Dust food colours: black and yellow (SK)
Metallic lustre dust food colour: silver (SK)
Icing sugar in a sugar shaker
Edible glue
Cooled, boiled water
A few drops of clear alcohol (e.g. vodka or gin)
2 sugar sticks

EQUIPMENT

35cm (14") square cake board
Large and small rolling pins
Pastry brush
Cake smoother
Palette knife
Serrated knife
Straight-bladed knife
Sable paintbrush: no. 2 (SK)
Dusting brush (SK)
10cm (4") circle cutter
Ball or bone tool
New, clean pan scourer
Piping nozzle: no. 2
A few cocktail sticks
Foam sheet
Foam pieces (for support)
Length of elastic thread
Template (see page 123)

Recipes and a baking chart can be found on pages 8 to 15

METHOD

Covering the Board

1. Knead 500g (1lb 1$^3/_4$oz) of mid-blue sugarpaste until soft and pliable. Dampen the cake board with a little cooled, boiled water, roll out the sugarpaste on a non-stick board or work surface dusted with a sprinkling of icing sugar to prevent sticking and cover the cake board. Rub the surface with a cake smoother and trim away the excess paste from around the edge.

Silhouette

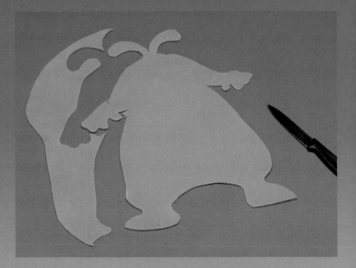

2. To allow drying time, make the pastillage shadow of the Were-rabbit next, using the template. Thinly roll out the dark grey pastillage, place the template down onto it and cut around the shape, using the cake smoother to hold the template in place. Rub gently around the cut edge to soften the edge and remove any crumbs and then place flat on a foam sheet to dry.

3. For the moon, thinly roll out the pale yellow pastillage and cut a circle using the 10cm (4") circle cutter. Smooth the edge and set aside to dry on the foam sheet. To make the wood effect pole, thinly roll out the brown pastillage into a sausage measuring 8cm (3") in length, mark lines over the surface to create a wood grain effect and allow to dry.

Covering the Cake

4. Trim the crust from the cake and level the top. Cut a layer in the cake and sandwich back together with buttercream. Spread buttercream on the underside of the cake and place centrally on the cake board. Spread a layer over the surface of the cake to help the sugarpaste stick.

5. Roll out the remaining mid-blue sugarpaste and cover the cake completely, stretching out any pleats and smoothing down and around the shape. Trim away any excess paste from around the base. Smooth the surface with a cake smoother.

Accessories

6. Make the torch next using a small ball of black modelling paste. Roll a fat sausage and then roll one half thinner for the handle and round off the opposite end. Press the rounded end down on the work surface to flatten. Rub the flat area with a little silver metallic food dust and set aside to dry.

7. To make the sack, roll the grey/brown modelling paste into a teardrop and push into the point to open up the top of the sack. Smooth the edge and pull up one side ready for Gromit's hand. Texture the surface by pressing the sack down onto the scourer and then set aside.

Wallace and Gromit

8. To make Wallace's outfit, roll just under 30g (1oz) of blue/grey modelling paste into a sausage and make a cut up to halfway to separate the legs. Pinch down both sides to remove the ridges. Bend the legs into the pose, pinching up the knees slightly, and mark fabric effect pleats with a cocktail stick.

9. For the sleeves, split 5g (just under ¼oz) of blue/grey modelling paste in half, roll two sausages and hollow out one end of each with the end of a paintbrush. Bend halfway and pinch out the paste at the back for elbows. Stick the sleeves in place with edible glue and smooth the join closed. To remove the join completely, rub gently with a little icing sugar on your fingers. Push a sugar stick down through the top of the body until only a little is protruding to support the head later. Lay flat and set aside to dry.

10. Use blue/grey modelling paste to make the detailing to Wallace's outfit. Thinly roll out the paste and cut a strip for the belt, yoke and pocket. Cut out tiny buttons using the piping nozzle. Paint these buttons with silver metallic food dust mixed to a paint consistency with a tiny amount of clear alcohol and paint a small buckle on the front of the belt.

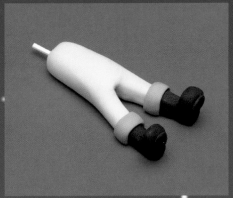

11. For the boots, split 10g (¹/₄oz) of black modelling paste into four and roll into sausage shapes, bending halfway to create the foot shape. Pinch out the heels at the back and flatten the top. Shape four flattened sausages into soles, pressing one end down further to widen the toe area. Stick a pair of boots onto Wallace's trousers with a flattened sausage of mid-brown modelling paste wrapped round the top of each to hold them securely. Set the second pair of boots aside for Gromit later.

12. To make Gromit's body and legs, roll 20g (³/₄oz) of palest brown modelling paste into a sausage shape and make a small cut to separate the legs. Smooth at the front and back to remove the ridges and cut the legs straight at the bottom so the boots fit neatly.

Smooth the top of the body upwards to narrow slightly and push a sugar stick down through the top, as before. Secure the boots to the legs, again using a strip of mid-brown modelling paste to hold them securely, and lay flat to dry.

13. Make Wallace and Gromit's heads next, following the instructions in the How to Model Wallace and Gromit section (see pages 24 to 26). Use half the flesh modelling paste for Wallace and 5g (just under ¹/₄oz) of palest brown for Gromit. When the heads are complete, slice off the top of each one so the caps will sit neatly. Make a small hole in Wallace's neck and at the bottom of Gromit's head ready for the sugar stick and then set aside to dry.

14. To create a shadow on the cake, brush the top of the cake at the back and down the sides with black dust food colour using the dusting brush. Apply the colour in a circular movement, building up dense colour little by little, fading out towards the edges. Add a little shadow on either side of the cake board.

15. When the pastillage silhouette is completely dry, brush the surface with black dust food colour, excluding the shoulders and outline, then dust these areas with yellow dust food colour. Using

a little royal icing, stick the moon at the back and leave to dry.

16. Stick the silhouette in place at the back of the cake using royal icing. Hold the piece for a few moments until secure by pressing against the lower part with the cake smoother. Stick the figures in position against the pastillage silhouette with dabs of royal icing, holding for a few moments until secure. Make sure the figures are well balanced. Use pieces of foam for support if necessary.

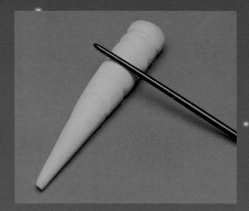

17. Using the remaining palest brown modelling paste, make Gromit's arms following the instructions in the How to Model Wallace and Gromit section (see page 26) and smooth the join closed as before. Stick the sack into one hand and secure his head in position.

18. For Wallace's hands, split the remaining flesh modelling paste in half and follow the modelling instructions (see page 25). Mould the hands into their pose with one holding onto the pole and the other holding the torch, then stick each wrist securely into the sleeves using edible glue. Use pieces of foam for support if necessary.

19. Push Wallace's head down onto the sugar stick and secure at the base with a little edible glue. Thinly roll out a little blue modelling paste and cut a strip for the collar. To make the caps, split 5g (just under ¹/₄oz) of blue modelling paste in half. Roll one half into a ball, cut in half and mark a cross on the top of each one using a knife. Split the remaining piece in half and model two flattened oval shapes for each cap peak. Assemble each cap in place, smoothing the peaks up at the front.

Carrot

20. To make the carrot, roll the orange modelling paste into a long teardrop shape and roll the paintbrush handle over the surface to indent markings. Push the end of the paintbrush into the full end to make a small hole. Dilute a tiny amount of brown paste food colour with a little cooled, boiled water to make a translucent colour wash and paint this over the carrot.

21. Tie a length of elastic thread to the pole and then around the carrot and stick the carrot in position with a little edible glue. Split the green modelling paste in half and model flattened teardrop shapes for leaves. Pinch around the outside edge of each to thin and frill the leaves and mark the vein down the centre using the back of a knife. Stick the leaves into the top of the carrot with a little edible glue.

Remember to remove the elastic thread before the cake is served.

ANTI-PESTO
S.W.A.T. TEAM

"You've saved the day!"

The Flying Sidecar

Here's Gromit in the motorcycle's sidecar, designed by good old Wallace to transform into an aeroplane in case it should become detached. The plane even comes complete with a porridge gun!

MATERIALS

30cm (12") square sponge cake

450g (1lb) buttercream

Sugarpaste: 45g (1^1/$_2$oz) black, 250g (8^3/$_4$oz) blue/green, 1kg (2lb 3^1/$_4$oz) red and 250g (8^3/$_4$oz) white

Modelling paste: 145g (5oz) black, 30g (1oz) brown, small ball of golden brown, 45g (1^1/$_2$oz) grey, 135g (4^3/$_4$oz) palest brown and small ball of white

Metallic lustre dust food colours: gold and silver (SK)

Icing sugar in a sugar shaker

Edible glue

A few drops of cooled, boiled water

10-15ml (2-3tsp) clear alcohol (e.g. vodka or gin)

Sugar stick

EQUIPMENT

40cm (16") round board

Large and small rolling pins

Pastry brush

Cake smoother

Palette knife

Serrated carving knife

Straight-bladed cutting knife

Sable paintbrushes: nos. 1 and 2 (SK)

0.5cm (^{1}/$_8$"), 1.5cm (^{1}/$_2$"), 2.5cm (1"), 3cm (1^1/$_4$"), 6cm (2^1/$_2$"), 8cm (3") and 10cm (4") and circle cutters

7cm (2^3/$_4$") square cutter

Bone or ball tool

Plain piping nozzles: nos. 1, 2 and 3

A few cocktail sticks

Foam pieces (for support)

Recipes and a baking chart can be found on pages 8 to 15

METHOD

Covering the Cake and Board

1. Knead the white and blue/green sugarpaste separately until soft and pliable. Knead the colours together to create a streaked effect and then roll out the sugarpaste on a non-stick board or work surface dusted with a sprinkling of icing sugar to prevent sticking and cover the cake board. Rub the surface with a cake smoother, trim away any excess paste from around the edge and set aside to dry.

2. Trim the crust from the cake and slice the top flat. Cut the cake exactly in half and stack one half on top of the other. Trim to narrow and taper both ends and then round the top so the cake slopes down to the base. Carve out the seat area just beyond halfway, cutting down to the first layer and taking out a hole using the 6cm (2^1/$_2$") circle cutter. Trim around the bottom of the cake so it curves in slightly.

3. Spread buttercream on the underside of the cake and position it centrally on the cake board. Sandwich the layers together with buttercream, then spread a layer over the surface of the cake to help the sugarpaste stick.

4. To cover the cake, roll out 625g (1lb 6oz) of red sugarpaste and cover

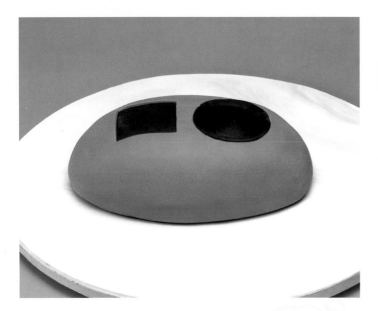

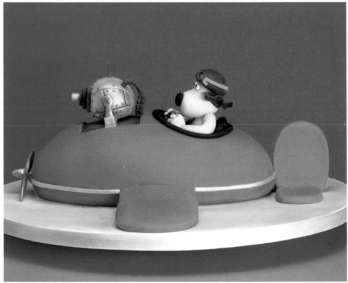

the cake completely, stretching out any pleats and smoothing downwards and around the shape. Trim away the excess paste from around the base. Cut out a circle from the seat area using the 8cm (3") circle cutter and a square from the front using the square cutter. Thinly roll out a little black sugarpaste and cut a square using the square cutter and a circle using the 10cm (4") circle cutter to cover the smaller circle, pushing the excess paste down into the hole.

Plane

5. For the wings, split 315g (11oz) of red sugarpaste in half and roll into two fat sausage shapes. Press down onto each one at an angle using the cake smoother, and then cut the thicker end straight. Stick each wing in place pushed up against the side of the plane.

6. For the upright fin, roll 35g (1¹⁄₄oz) of red sugarpaste into an oval shape and press flat with the cake smoother. Cut the bottom straight and set aside. For the tail fins, split the remaining

red paste in half and repeat. Assemble at the back of the plane.

7. Roll a thin sausage of black modelling paste to edge the top of the cockpit. For the back of the seat, roll 10g (¹⁄₄oz) into a sausage, taper each end, flatten slightly and then indent three lines fanning from the centre. Stick in position at the back of the opening.

8. Stick a small ball of grey modelling paste onto the front of the plane. Thinly roll out some more grey modelling paste and cut strips to decorate the plane. For the propeller, roll a

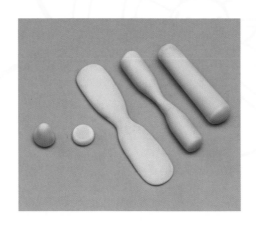

sausage from 10g (¹⁄₄oz) of paste and roll thinner in the centre. Press down with the cake smoother, add a small teardrop in the centre and set aside to dry.

9. Thinly roll out more grey paste and cut a strip for the base of the gun support, the width of the black square. Cut two small oblongs for each end and then shape two pieces for the gun support, pressing each one flat. Set these pieces aside to dry.

Porridge Gun

10. For the gun, roll 90g (3oz) of black modelling paste into a ball and indent lines with a knife. Roll a sausage for the gun muzzle and indent the centre to hollow out. Thinly roll out a little black modelling paste and cut three circles for the front using the 3cm (1¹⁄₄"), 2.5cm (1") and 1.5cm (¹⁄₂") circle cutters. Assemble together and then cut a circle from the centre using the 0.5cm (¹⁄₈") circle cutter. Stick the gun muzzle into the centre.

11. Assemble the support pieces either side, sticking them on the gun sides. Stick a black circle on each side for the screw heads and mark each one down the centre with a knife. Push the end of a paintbrush into the back of the gun twice to make holes for the hoses. Split 5g (just under $1/_4$oz) of black modelling paste in half and roll into two sausages. Indent each one by rolling over the surface with a cocktail stick. Stick these in position, curving up and out of the indented holes.

12. For the bolts on the gun, thinly roll out 5g (just under $1/_4$oz) of black modelling paste and allow to firm for a few moments. Dust the surface with icing sugar and then cut repeatedly into the paste with the no. 3 piping nozzle, letting the circles collect in the nozzle. When you

have enough, tip out the circles and stick them in place over the gun one at a time, picking each up with the damp glue brush.

13. To make the target finder, roll a tiny sausage of black modelling paste and round off one end. Press this rounded end flat and cut out four circles using the no. 2 piping nozzle, then set aside to dry. Push a hole into the top of the gun where the target finder will be positioned later.

14. Roll a small sausage of black modelling paste and round off each end for the steering wheel. Bend the

two ends up and press the top of each end flat. Stick in position at the front of the opening with small, flattened circles of red modelling paste for the buttons.

Gromit

15. To make Gromit, roll 45g (1$1/_2$oz) of palest brown modelling paste into an oval shape and push down into the seat opening. Push a sugar stick down through the body until only a little is protruding to help hold his head in place. Make Gromit's head using 60g (2oz) of paste and split 30g (1oz) in half to make the two arms, following instructions in the How to Model Wallace and Gromit section (see page 25 to 26).

16. Stick his two arms in position holding onto the steering wheel. Blend the join at the shoulder using a little edible glue and then rub gently over the join with a little icing sugar on your fingers to remove the join completely. Cut off the top of Gromit's head at a slight backwards angle, ready for the helmet.

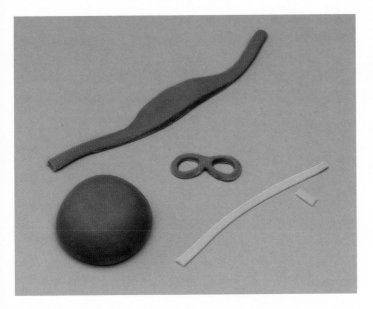

17. To make the helmet, roll 25g (just over ³/₄oz) of brown modelling paste into a ball and press down on the work surface to flatten the bottom. Pinch gently around the outside edge, making it slightly larger than the top of Gromit's head.

18. For the goggles, roll a small sausage of brown modelling paste and roll further in the centre to narrow. Press the cake smoother down to flatten the paste. Cut out the centre of each using the 0.5cm (¹/₈") circle cutter and reshape slightly to elongate the holes using the end of a paintbrush. Stick the goggles in position on the front of the helmet and add a thin strip of golden brown for the strap.

19. Stick the helmet on top of Gromit's head. Thinly roll out the remaining brown modelling paste and cut two strips for the helmet straps. Stick each one in place and support with pieces of foam if necessary. Mix some metallic silver lustre dust with clear alcohol and paint into the eye area of the goggles for a glass effect. Stick the propeller in position and paint silver along the edging around the plane.

To Finish

20. Mix some gold metallic lustre dust with clear alcohol and paint the gun, bolts, muzzle and screws. Stick the target in position.

21. Dilute a little blue/green paste food colour with a few drops of clear alcohol and paint the cloud effect on the cake board around the plane using a no. 1 paintbrush.

"Hang on, old chum!"

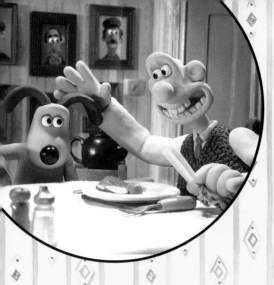

Tea Time

Wallace and Gromit are ready for a tea time treat of cheese, cheese and more cheese – including Wensleydale, of course! Not forgetting the crackers and a nice cup of tea.

MATERIALS

30cm (12") square sponge cake

Sugarpaste: 900g (2lb) white and 200g (7oz) dark green

Modelling paste: tiny piece of black, 10g ($^1/_4$oz) blue, 15g ($^1/_2$oz) brown, just under 5g ($^1/_8$oz) cream, 35g ($1^1/_4$oz) dark brown, 45g ($1^1/_2$oz) dark green, just under 5g ($^1/_8$oz) dark yellow, 35g ($1^1/_4$oz) flesh, 15g ($^1/_2$oz) golden brown, 10g ($^1/_4$oz) lemon, 10g ($^1/_4$oz) mauve, 15g ($^1/_2$oz) orange, 30g (1oz) pale blue, 60g (2oz) palest brown, just under 5g ($^1/_8$oz) red and 60g (2oz) white

Pastillage: 225g (8oz) brown

Paste food colours: black and dark green (SK)

Metallic lustre dust food colour: silver (SK)

Icing sugar in a sugar shaker

Edible glue

Cooled, boiled water

2 sugar sticks

EQUIPMENT

30cm (12") square cake board

Large and small rolling pins

Pastry brush

Cake smoother

Palette knife

Serrated carving knife

Straight-bladed cutting knife

Sable paintbrush: no. 2 (SK)

Small blossom cutter

2.5cm (1") and 4cm ($1^1/_2$") circle cutters

1.5cm ($^1/_2$") and 5cm (2") square cutters

Bone or ball tool

Piping nozzles: nos. 1 and 3

A few cocktail sticks

Ruler

Foam sheet

Foam pieces (for support)

Templates (see page 122)

Recipes and a baking chart can be found on pages 8 to 15

METHOD

Covering the Board

1. Knead 200g (7oz) of white sugarpaste until soft and pliable. Using a sprinkling of icing sugar to prevent sticking, roll out the paste on a non-stick board or work surface and cut eighteen squares using the large square cutter. Roll out the dark green sugarpaste and repeat. Dampen the cake board with a little cooled, boiled water and position the squares on the cake board in a chequerboard pattern. Rub the surface with a cake smoother.

2. Dilute a little dark green paste food colour with a little cooled, boiled water to make a translucent colour wash. Using a pastry brush, paint over the surface of the white tiles, keeping the brush quite dry to gain a pale, streaked effect.

Chairs

3. To allow for drying time, make the chair pieces next using the brown pastillage. Roll out the pastillage and cut out the chair pieces one at a time using the templates. Reserve the trimmings for use later. Mark lines by indenting with the side of a ruler and create a wood grain effect by marking with the tip of a knife. The pastillage will harden very quickly and when this happens, stick the seat onto the chair and then place on the foam sheet to dry completely.

Covering the Cake

4. Trim the crust from the cake and slice the top flat. Cut a 2.5cm (1") strip from opposite sides of the cake and then cut the cake in half lengthways to make two oblong cakes measuring 20cm x 15cm (8" x 6"). Cut a layer in each and sandwich all layers one on top of the other using buttercream. Spread a layer on the underside of the cake and position on the cake board at a slight angle. Spread a layer of buttercream over the surface of the cake to help the sugarpaste stick.

5. Roll out 500g (1lb 1³/₄oz) of white sugarpaste and cover the cake completely, stretching out pleats and smoothing downwards and around the shape. Trim away the excess paste from around the base. To create a shadow effect, dilute a little black paste food colour with a few drops of water to achieve a watercolour paint consistency and paint a streaked shadow around the bottom of the cake only.

6. For the tablecloth, thinly roll out 160g (5¹/₂oz) of white sugarpaste and cut an oblong measuring 25cm x 30cm (10" x 12"). Cut a curve at each corner. Moisten the cake with a little edible glue and then lift the paste and lay it over the top of the cake, encouraging the paste to form pleats around the sides. Press the surface of the paste flat against the cake where the chairs will be inserted.

7. For the small, checked tablecloth, thinly roll out the pale blue modelling paste and cut squares using the small square cutter. Cover these over with clingfilm to prevent the paste from drying out. Thinly roll out the remaining white sugarpaste and then stick the blue squares over the surface using as little edible glue as possible. Press on the surface with a cake smoother. Make sure the sugarpaste is loose on the work surface and then roll over the surface with the rolling pin to inlay the pattern. Cut around the outside edge, making the measurement around 16cm (6¹/₂") square, and position on the cake, securing with a little edible glue.

Tableware

8. Make all the tableware using the various coloured modelling paste. Cut plates and saucers using the circle cutters. To indent the centre, place on the foam sheet and press a circle cutter in the centre, pushing down into the foam. For the dotty pattern on the white plate, cut tiny circles with the no. 1 piping nozzle

and stick in place using edible glue and a fine paintbrush.

9. To make a cup, shape a teardrop and push into the full end with the end of a paintbrush, winding it around to open up the paste. Pinch around the top edge and push down on the point to flatten the base. Roll a tiny sausage for the handle and secure in place with edible glue. Roll a small ball of golden brown modelling paste and drop into the cup for the tea.

10. Cut out small squares for crackers and make marks in the top of each using the tip of a cocktail stick.

11. To make the jug, roll an oval of mauve modelling paste, push into the top and pinch the spout. Fill the top with white paste for the milk. Decorate with circles of lemon coloured paste cut from the no. 3 piping nozzle.

12. For the cheese dome, cut a small oblong of lemon modelling paste and make the top slightly angled. Cut a larger rectangle for the base. For the handle, loop a small sausage of paste and stick this onto the top. To decorate the

side, roll out some blue modelling paste and cut out tiny flowers and circles using the blossom cutter and the no. 1 piping nozzle. Stick in place with edible glue.

13. Model the teapot on a small, flattened circular stand using the dark brown modelling paste. For the spout, roll a tiny tapered sausage and push the end of a paintbrush into the narrow end to open it up. For the rim and lid, stick on flattened circles and a ball.

14. For the knife, roll a small piece of the pastillage trimmings into a sausage and press down halfway with the flat of a knife. Cut the blade straight. Brush silver metallic food dust over the surface of the blade and buff gently with the paintbrush.

15. For the cheese board, roll out some golden brown modelling paste and cut an oblong, then soften and round off each corner. Use the dark yellow, cream, orange and red modelling paste for the cheeses and indent holes in a wedge using the end of a paintbrush.

16. Using edible glue, stick the chairs in position, pushing the seats gently but securely into the cake covering.

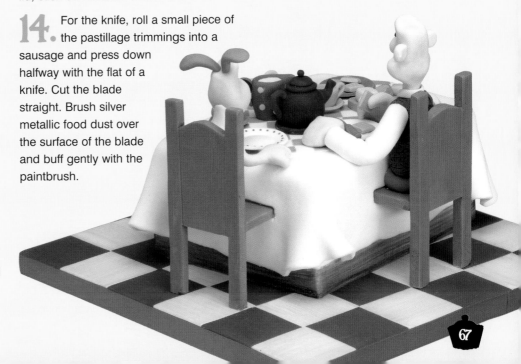

Gromit

17. Make Gromit from palest brown modelling paste following the instructions given in the How to Model Wallace and Gromit section (see pages 25 to 26). Use 35g (1¼oz) for his body, split 15g (½oz) in half for his two arms and use the remainder for his head.

Wallace

18. For Wallace's trousers, roll the remaining brown modelling paste into a ball and this stick onto the chair and against the tablecloth. For his pullover, roll the dark green modelling paste into a teardrop shape and press down on the point to flatten an area for Wallace's head. Press the base down on the work surface to flatten. Press the flat of a knife into the chest to mark a 'v' shape and push in either side to indent armholes.

19. Using the back of a knife, mark a band around the 'v' neck and around each armhole, and then roll the knife over the surface to indent lines. Use a cocktail stick to mark the knitted pattern. For his shirt, roll a pea-sized amount of white modelling paste into a teardrop and press flat. Stick in place in the 'v' of the pullover. Push a sugar stick down into the top until a little is protruding to help hold the head in place. Stick the pullover onto the trousers and against the tablecloth.

20. For Wallace's sleeves, split 30g (1oz) of white modelling paste in half and roll into sausage shapes. To make a space for the hands to be attached, indent into the end of each sleeve using the end of a paintbrush. Bend each arm halfway and then stick in position resting on the table.

21. For Wallace's hands, split 15g (½oz) of flesh modelling paste in half and follow the instructions in the How to Model Wallace and Gromit section (see page 25). Stick in position with one hand holding a cracker. For his

tie, roll a tiny tapered sausage of red modelling paste and then model a teardrop shape for the knot and secure in place.

22. Make Wallace's head using the remaining flesh modelling paste, following the instructions in the modelling section (see page 24). Push the head down onto the sugar stick and secure at the base with edible glue. Roll out and cut a tiny strip of white for the collar, wrap around his neck and stick in place to hide the join.

"I'm just crackers about cheese!"

Dogfight

This design was inspired by the dogfight in the fairground planes between Gromit and Philip in the film 'The Curse of the Were-rabbit'. As usual, and rightly so, the sharp-witted Gromit wins the day!

MATERIALS

25cm (10") square sponge cake
500g (1lb 1^3/$_4$oz) buttercream
Sugarpaste: 400g (14oz) black and 1.8kg (4lb) pale ivory
Modelling paste: just under 5g (^{1}/$_8$oz) black, 240g (8^1/$_2$oz) blue, just under 5g (^{1}/$_8$oz) brown, just under 5g (^{1}/$_8$oz) golden brown, 20g (^{3}/$_4$oz) pale grey, 10g (^{1}/$_4$oz) palest brown, 240g (8^1/$_2$oz) red and just under 5g (^{1}/$_8$oz) white
Dust food colour: black (SK)
Metallic lustre dust food colour: silver (SK)
Moonbeams lustre dust food colour: sapphire (SK)
Icing sugar in a sugar shaker
Edible glue
A few drops of cooled, boiled water
5-10ml (1-2tsp) clear alcohol (e.g. vodka or gin)
2 sugar sticks

EQUIPMENT

30cm (12") square cake board
Large and small rolling pins
Cake smoother
Palette knife
Serrated carving knife
Straight-bladed cutting knife
Sable paintbrush: no. 2 (SK)
Dusting brush (SK)
3cm (1^1/$_4$") and 4cm (1^1/$_2$") circle cutters
New, clean pan scourer
Plain piping nozzle: no. 1
A few cocktail sticks
Ruler
Foam pieces (for support)

Recipes and a baking chart can be found on pages 8 to 15

METHOD

Covering the Cake and Board

1. Knead the black sugarpaste until soft and pliable. Roll out the sugarpaste on a non-stick board or work surface dusted with a sprinkling of icing sugar to prevent sticking and cover the cake board. Trim away the excess paste from around the edge and rub the surface with a cake smoother. Set aside to dry.

2. Trim the crust from the cake and slice the top flat. Cut a generous 8cm (3") strip from the cake and place this on top of the cake, level with the back. Cut layers in both cakes and sandwich all layers together with buttercream. Spread buttercream on the underside of the cake and position on the cake board, slightly off-centre.

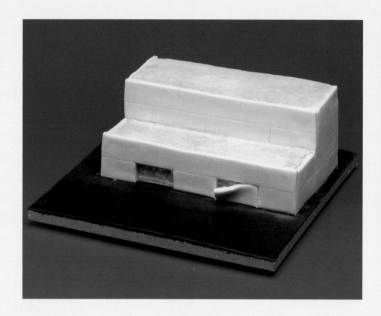

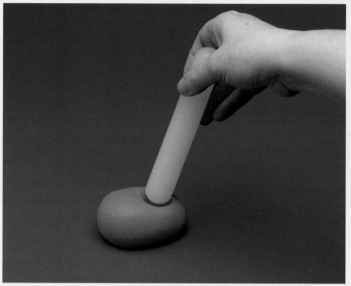

3. Roll out 260g (9oz) of pale ivory sugarpaste and cut a piece to cover the back of the cake. Stick the paste in place and smooth over the surface with a cake smoother. Texture the stone effect by gently pressing the scourer over the surface. Make sure the cuts at each corner are straight and neat.

4. Using 260g (9oz) of the pale ivory sugarpaste, cover the sides next, securing the joins closed with a little edible glue and smoothing them with your finger. Cover the front area using a further 260g (9oz) of paste. Smooth the surface and texture as before. Cut out two windows measuring 5cm x 2.5cm (2" x 1") from the front of the cake and take out the sugarpaste. Thinly roll out the black sugarpaste trimmings and cut pieces to fill each window. To mark the brick pattern, place the ruler against the surface and score lines with a knife.

5. Using the remaining pale ivory sugarpaste, measure the top of the cake and cut pieces for both uncovered surfaces, making the pieces slightly larger than the cake. This cut edge

will show, so cut neatly and rub the edge gently with your fingertips. Build up the roof with two more layers, each one slightly larger than the last, to achieve a stepped effect. Using the pale ivory trimmings, cut thin strips for the windowpanes and to edge the top of each window.

Planes

6. To make the red plane, roll 185g (6½oz) of red modelling paste into an oval shape. Press into the centre to indent a hole just beyond halfway, smoothing around the edge to open up further. Stroke the sides at the back to elongate and narrow the oval slightly. Make another plane using blue modelling paste, then thinly roll out some grey paste and cover the bottom part of the blue plane only, trimming a straight line halfway up.

7. For the wing supports, roll some red modelling paste into a thin sausage and cut eight 2cm (¾") lengths. Repeat with blue modelling paste, this

time cutting four lengths. Set these aside to dry. To make each large wing, you will need to use 25g (just over ¾oz) of red or blue modelling paste. Roll this into a sausage measuring 9cm (3½") and press the cake smoother onto the surface to flatten. Cut out a semi-circle from one side using the 4cm (1½") circle cutter and set aside to dry.

8. Model the side wings next by flattening circles of red and blue modelling paste and cutting these in half. Make four red and two blue. Indent two small holes in each so the supports will hold them secure later.
Make the three pieces for each tail wing by modelling sausage

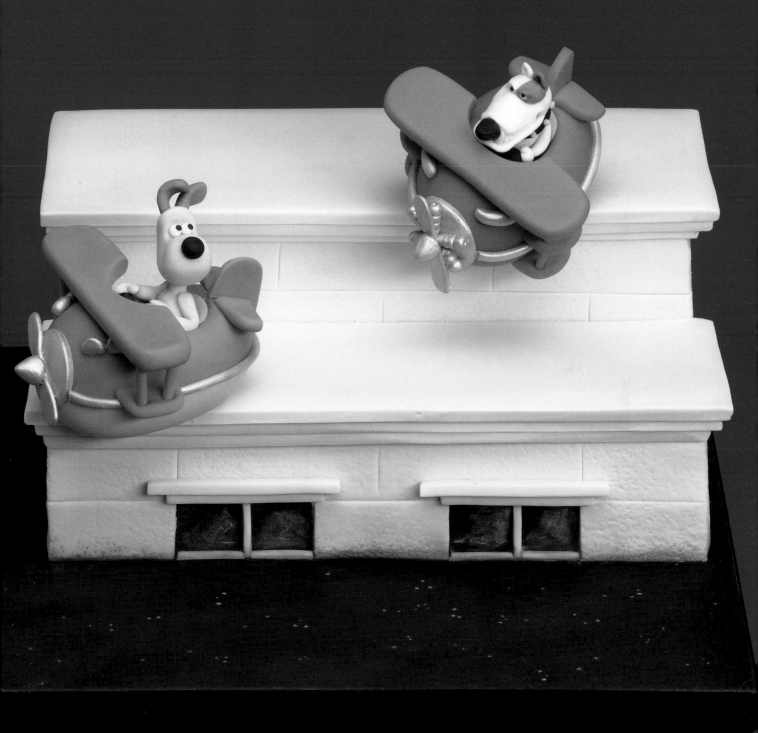

shapes and pressing flat. Cut one side of each to make them more angular.

9. Roll out 10g (¹/₄oz) of grey modelling paste and cut two circles for the front of each plane using the 3cm (1¹/₄") circle cutter. For the rotor blades, roll two small sausages of grey modelling paste and indent the centre of each by rolling the paste with your fingertip. Press down to flatten using the cake smoother and set aside.

10. For the red plane, roll six pea-sized amounts of grey modelling paste into teardrop shapes and indent rings around each by rolling over the surface with a cocktail stick. Indent the full end of each with the tip of a no. 1 piping nozzle and then stick in place around the circle on the front.

11. Split the golden brown modelling paste in half and model small, flattened circles for the seat backs. To make the steering wheels, roll pea-sized sausages of black modelling paste and indent the centre to round off each end. Bend into a curve and stick in place in each plane with edible glue.

12. Roll very thin sausages of grey modelling paste to edge the cockpit of each plane. Make small semi-circles to decorate either side at the front on the blue plane and curved teardrop shapes to decorate the red plane. Model two pea-sized teardrop shapes of grey and stick in position on top of each rotor blade, then stick the blades in position with edible glue.

13. Mix some silver metallic lustre dust with a little clear alcohol to the consistency of paint. Paint the grey

areas on each plane, paint a little over each window on the cake for a glass effect and add tiny dots and stars in clusters over the cake board.

Gromit

14. Model Gromit following the instructions in the How to Model Wallace and Gromit section (see pages 25 to 26). Use 10g (¹/₄oz) of palest brown modelling paste and use one half for his body and arms, and the other half for his head. Cut the bottom part off his body so he sits comfortably inside the blue plane. Push a sugar stick down through his neck until a little is protruding to help hold the head in place.

Philip

15. Model Philip's body and arms using 5g (just under ¹/₄oz) of white modelling paste. Roll a teardrop shape for the body. For the arms, roll sausages of paste, round off each end, flatten slightly,

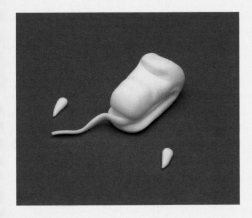

then push twice into one end of each to indent the paws. Stick the arms in place holding onto the steering wheel.

16. Model a small, flattened circle of black modelling paste for Philip's collar and stick on miniature teardrop shapes of grey for the spikes. Push a sugar stick down into the collar to help hold the head securely.

17. To make his head, roll 5g (just under ¼oz) of white modelling paste into a sausage. Pinch the top to create the eye area. For the mouth, roll a paintbrush handle around the front and sides to indent the paste. Pinch the top of the muzzle to narrow it slightly and roll a cocktail stick over the surface to mark lines. Using the handle of a paintbrush, stroke gently around the mouth and along the bottom edge to define the lips.

18. For the teeth, roll out and cut a very thin strip of white modelling paste to fit into the indented mouth. Mark the teeth using the tip of a knife. Model two tiny, pointed teardrop-shaped teeth for the front.

19. Stick a small, flattened piece of brown modelling paste onto the eye area for the patch, and then push the end of a paintbrush into the eye area to indent sockets. Model eyes in the same way as for Gromit and secure in place. Make two ears, one white, one brown by modelling tiny teardrop shapes and then indenting the centre of each. Model a black teardrop for his nose, press onto the point to flatten slightly and push up gently before securing in place.

To Finish

20. Mix a little icing sugar with the black dust food colour and brush a shadow effect around the base of the building. Brush some sapphire blue lustre dust in swirls over the cake board.

21. Assemble the plane wings when dry, using foam pieces for support if necessary. Stick in position on the cake, making sure the planes are secure and well balanced. If necessary, support with foam pieces until dry.

"Well come on lad! What are you waiting for?"

Gromit's Bathtime

I couldn't resist capturing this humorous scene of Gromit in his bath, complete with his endearing facial expression.

MATERIALS

18cm x 23cm (7" x 9") oval-shaped sponge cake

25cm (10") round sponge cake

625g (1lb 6oz) buttercream

Sugarpaste: 225g (8oz) brown, 225g (8oz) cream, 625g (1lb 6oz) grey, 900g (2lb) white

Modelling paste: 5g (just under $^1/_4$oz) black, 200g (7oz) bright blue, 30g (1oz) brown, 5g (just under $^1/_4$oz) orange, 625g (1lb 6oz) palest brown

Paste food colours: black, chestnut and golden brown (SK)

Metallic lustre dust food colour: silver (SK)

Icing sugar in a sugar shaker

Edible glue

15-30ml (1-2tbsp) cooled, boiled water

15ml (1tbsp) clear alcohol (e.g. vodka or gin)

3 sugar sticks

EQUIPMENT

30cm (12") square cake board

Large and small rolling pins

Pastry brush

Cake smoother

Palette knife

Serrated carving knife

Straight-bladed cutting knife

Sable paintbrush: no. 3 (SK)

Paint palette

7.5cm (3") square cutter

New, clean pan scourer

Bone or ball tool

A few cocktail sticks

Ruler

Recipes and a baking chart can be found on pages 8 to 15

METHOD

Carving and Covering the Cake

1. Knead the cream sugarpaste until soft and pliable. Roll out the sugarpaste on a non-stick board or work surface dusted with a sprinkling of icing sugar to prevent sticking and cut out eight 7.5cm (3") squares using a cutter. Repeat with the brown sugarpaste. Dampen the board with a little cooled, boiled water and cover the cake board in a chequerboard pattern. Rub the surface gently with a cake smoother to close the joins and then trim off any excess paste from around the edge.

2. For the paint effect, dilute a little golden brown paste food colour with a teaspoon of cooled, boiled water to make a colour wash. Paint the colour onto the covered board in a circular motion using the pastry brush. Set aside to dry.

Bath

3. Using a serrated knife, trim the crust from the oval-shaped cake and level the top. Trim the sides so that they taper inwards to the base by around 2cm ($^3/_4$"). Cut two layers in the cake and sandwich back together with buttercream. Spread buttercream on the underside of the cake and position centrally on the cake board.

Cover the surface with a thin layer of buttercream to help the sugarpaste stick.

4. To cover the sides of the cake, thus making the bath, roll out the grey sugarpaste and cut a strip measuring 63cm x 6cm (25" x $2^1/_2$"). Sprinkle this strip of sugarpaste with icing sugar to prevent sticking and roll into a spiral. Place the end against the front of the cake and unroll the paste around the sides, overlapping slightly at the join. Rub the surface with a cake smoother and then trim the overlap neatly. Indent a line around the base using the edge of a ruler. Using the grey sugarpaste trimmings, model little flattened circles for rivets to edge the overlap and roll a sausage for the handle, indenting down the centre only. Loop the handle and stick it in place, pressing each end flat with a rivet on the centre.

5. Mix the clear alcohol with silver lustre dust food colour to make a smooth paint consistency. Using a paintbrush, stipple the silver colour over the bath to create a metallic finish. Add a tiny amount of black paste food colour to the paint for darker areas near the joins and around the rivets.

6. Trim the crust from the remaining cake, keeping the rounded top where the cake has risen. Trim inwards around the base to round off further. To create an uneven surface, randomly cut out wedges and sandwich elsewhere with buttercream. Cut out a dip on the top of the cake ready for Gromit's body. Place this cake on top of the bath and spread the whole surface with buttercream, including the underneath edge to help the sugarpaste stick.

Gromit's Head and Body

7. To make Gromit's body, roll 300g ($10^1/_2$oz) of palest brown modelling paste into a teardrop shape and position this on top of the cake slightly towards the back, leaving room for his head.

8. To make his head, use 300g (10½oz) of palest brown and refer to the How to Model Wallace and Gromit section (see pages 25 to 26) for full instructions. Secure the head to the body, but do not make the ears yet.

Bubbles

9. To create the bubble effect, thickly roll out 650g (1lb 7oz) of white sugarpaste and texture the surface by pressing firmly with a new, clean pan scourer. Make a cut down the centre measuring approximately 15cm (6"). Place the cut directly over Gromit and lower the sugarpaste over him so that he comes through the opening. Smooth the paste around Gromit's body and around the cake, pinching the paste to make an uneven surface and tucking any excess underneath. Secure with a little edible glue. You will need to press the scourer over the surface once again where the texture has been lost.

10. Using the remaining white sugarpaste, make the overspill of bubbles down the sides of the cake, smoothing the join lines closed with a little edible glue and texturing as before. Model bubbles for Gromit's back. Reserve a little white sugarpaste to make bubble splashes and Gromit's eyes later.

Gromit's Ears and Tail

11. Push two sugar sticks into the top of Gromit's head, leaving at least 1-2cm (approximately ¾") protruding to help support the ears. Push another stick into the body for his tail. Split 25g (just over ¾oz) of brown modelling paste in half and use to make the ears (see page 26). Gently bend the ears over, push down onto the sugar stick to make a hole and then remove. Put aside and leave to set in their shape before sticking in position.

12. For Gromit's tail, roll a tapered sausage shape with a little brown modelling paste and stick in place over the sugar stick, securing with a little edible glue.

Scrubbing Brush

13. To make the scrubbing brush, first roll out 15g (½oz) of palest brown modelling paste and cut an oblong measuring 5cm x 1cm (2" x ⅜") for the bristles. Make uneven cuts in this oblong, flicking the paste out around the bottom. Shape the remaining palest brown paste into an oval shape for the handle and stick in place on top of the bristles using edible glue.

14. Dilute a little golden brown and chestnut paste food colours separately with a few drops of cooled, boiled water. Using a no. 3 sable paintbrush, paint a wash of golden brown over the bristles and a streaked effect using the chestnut colour over the handle.

Towel

15. For the towel, thinly roll out the orange modelling paste, cut a narrow strip measuring 15cm (6") in length and set aside. Thinly roll out the bright blue modelling paste and cut an oblong measuring approximately 15cm x 25cm (6" x 10"). Stick the orange strip onto the towel and texture the whole surface using the scourer. Fold the towel lengthways and then roll it up and stick in place on the cake board.

To Finish

16. Roll two balls of white sugarpaste for the eyes and then stick on two flattened circles of black modelling paste for pupils. Roll the remaining black modelling paste into a ball and stick in place for his nose, then smooth and flatten the paste around the edge. Stick the ears in place using edible glue.

17. Model all the bubble splashes from the remaining white sugarpaste, texturing as before, and secure in place with edible glue.

"You're a total knockout!"

Pop Art

These fun, modern images of Wallace and Gromit are extremely quick and easy to make. The design can also be adapted as they look just as good side by side, or even on their own separate cake boards.

MATERIALS

2 x 15cm (6") square sponge cakes

450g (1lb) buttercream

Sugarpaste: 500g (1lb 1$\frac{3}{4}$oz) black, 550g (1lb 3$\frac{1}{2}$oz) green, 15g ($\frac{1}{2}$oz) lilac, 60g (2oz) white, 550g (1lb 3$\frac{1}{2}$oz) yellow

Icing sugar in a sugar shaker

Edible glue

A few drops of cooled, boiled water

EQUIPMENT

25cm x 35cm (10" x 14") oblong cake board

2 x 15cm (6") square cake cards

Large rolling pin

Pastry brush

Cake smoother

Palette knife

Serrated knife

Straight-bladed cutting knife

Sable paintbrush: no. 2 (SK)

Templates (see page 124 to 125)

Recipes and a baking chart can be found on pages 8 to 15

METHOD

Covering the Board and Cakes

1. Dampen the cake board with a little cooled, boiled water. Knead the black sugarpaste until soft and pliable and roll out on a non-stick board or work surface dusted with a sprinkling of icing sugar to prevent sticking. Cover the cake board completely and smooth the surface with a cake smoother. Trim away the excess paste from around the edge and reserve the trimmings.

2. Trim the crust from each cake and level the tops. Slice two layers in each cake and sandwich back together with buttercream. Spread buttercream on the underside and place each cake on a cake card. Spread a layer of buttercream over the surface to help the sugarpaste stick.

3. Roll out the yellow sugarpaste and cover one of the cakes completely, stretching out pleats and smoothing downwards and around the shape. Rub the surface with a cake smoother and then trim away any excess paste from around the base. Cover the second cake in the same way using the green sugarpaste.

Pop Art Pictures

4. Trace the images from the template onto a sheet of greaseproof paper. Thinly roll out some white sugarpaste and cut out the Wallace and Gromit shapes. Place these centrally on top of each cake and smooth over the surface with a cake smoother to remove air pockets. Brush a little edible glue around the outside edge to stick the shapes in place.

5. Thinly roll out the lilac sugarpaste and the green and yellow sugarpaste trimmings and cut out the shapes from the templates, this time making the shapes slightly smaller than the templates. Thinly roll out the white trimmings and cut out Wallace's mouth. Place the pieces in position, smooth and secure as before.

6. Roll thin, uneven sausages of black sugarpaste a little at a time and use to outline each image. Secure the outlines in place with a little edible glue. Make the sausages much finer to outline Wallace's teeth. Roll a pea-sized ball of black for Gromit's nose and flatten, then cut out a small hole using the tip of a knife. Secure in place.

To Finish

7. To edge around the base of each cake, roll long, uneven sausages of black sugarpaste, stick in place with a little edible glue and then press flat against the cake sides using the cake smoother.

8. When complete, position each cake on the cake board and secure in place with a little edible glue.

"Happy birthday chuck!"

Mini Cakes

These stylish mini cakes decorated with characters from A Close Shave are perfect for any small gathering. For larger celebrations, you could serve these individual cakes to your guests to complement a larger cake.

MATERIALS

6 x 5cm (2") cube sponge cakes

175g (6oz) buttercream

Sugarpaste: 145g (5oz) blue, 145g (5oz) cream, 145g (5oz) lilac, 145g (5oz) pale green, 145g (5oz) pale peach and 145g (5oz) pink

Modelling paste: 20g ($^3/_4$oz) black, 10g ($^1/_4$oz) brown, 20g ($^3/_4$oz) flesh, pea-sized amount of orange, 10g ($^1/_4$oz) pale brown, pea-sized amount palest blue, 10g ($^1/_4$oz) palest brown, 5g (just under $^1/_4$oz) red and 10g ($^1/_4$oz) white

Edible glue

Icing sugar in a sugar shaker

A few drops of cooled, boiled water

EQUIPMENT

6 x 7cm (2$^3/_4$") square cake cards

Small rolling pin

Pastry brush

Cake smoother

Palette knife

Serrated knife

Straight-bladed cutting knife

Sable paintbrush: no. 2 (SK)

Ball or bone tool

A few cocktail sticks

Templates (see page 124 to 125)

Recipes and a baking chart can be found on pages 8 to 15

METHOD

Covering the Cakes and Cards

1. Dampen a cake card with a little cooled, boiled water. Knead 20g ($^3/_4$oz) of the pale green sugarpaste until soft and pliable. Roll out the sugarpaste on a non-stick board or work surface dusted with a sprinkling of icing sugar to prevent sticking, cover the cake card and smooth the surface with a cake smoother. Trim away the excess paste from around the edge and set aside to dry. Cover the remaining cake cards using blue, pink, pale peach, lilac and cream coloured sugarpaste and set aside to dry. Keep the remaining coloured sugarpaste airtight.

2. Trim the crust from each cake and level the tops. Spread buttercream on the underside and place each cake centrally on a covered cake card. Spread a layer of buttercream over the surface of the cakes to help the sugarpaste stick.

3. Using the remaining pale green, blue, pink, pale peach, lilac and cream sugarpaste, cover each of the cakes in a different colour to the cake card (following the main picture as a guide), smoothing the paste down and around the shape. Smooth the surface with a cake smoother and trim away any excess from around the base, taking care not to damage the covered card.

4. Trace all the images from the template onto a sheet of greaseproof paper.

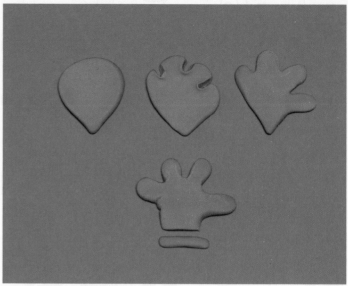

Wallace

5. Work on the green cake on the cream card. Using the template, cut out the image of Wallace's face from flesh modelling paste and smooth around the edge with your fingertip to remove the ridge. Indent a small curve for the mouth using the paintbrush handle. Fill the corner of the mouth with a tiny piece of dark pink modelling paste and then cut a tiny strip of white and indent three times for the teeth. Model a pea-sized ear, secure in place and indent the centre using a ball or bone tool. Roll a ball for the nose, secure in place with edible glue and flatten slightly. Add tiny balls for the eyes, stick a small, black pupil on each, then finish with a minute white highlight on each eye.

'Feathers' McGraw

6. Work on the blue cake on the pink card. Using the template, cut a small square of black modelling paste and smooth around the edge to soften the ridge. Roll a pea-sized piece of orange modelling paste into a ball and press flat. Cut this in half and use one half for the beak. Roll two tiny white balls for the eyes and press flat. Stick the eyes in place and add black pupils and a tiny white highlight, as before. For his rubber glove 'hat', model a teardrop shape from red modelling paste and roll flat. Push the end of a paintbrush into the paste three times along the top to separate the fingers, and then gently round off the edges. Mark little pleats with a cocktail stick. Cut the hat straight at the bottom, secure in place and roll a sausage for the rim.

Preston

7. Work on the pink cake on the blue card. Using the template, cut out Preston's head from pale brown modelling paste and indent the eye area by rolling a paintbrush handle into the surface. Roll a sausage to edge the bottom. Make two teardrop shapes for the ears and indent the centre of each using the end of a paintbrush. Stick on a black, oval-shaped nose with a little white highlight. Model two white eyes with tiny black pupils.

Shaun the Sheep

8. Work on the pale peach cake on the lilac card. Using the template, cut out Shaun's head from black modelling paste, smoothing the edge as before. Indent nostrils with the end of a paintbrush. Model his ear and stick on a tiny strip of white for a highlight. Model eyes with a highlight as before and shape different sized flattened balls of white modelling paste for the wool.

Wendolene

9. Work on the lilac cake on the pale peach card. Using the template, cut out Wendolene's face shape from flesh modelling paste. Indent the mouth area in the same way as for Wallace, filling the space with a flattened sausage of white

modelling paste. Indent the teeth using a knife. Model the nose from a ball of flesh modelling paste (as for Wallace) and stick on a flattened ball for the ear. Model the eyes with brown pupils and add a little white highlight on the top. For the eye shadow, make tiny tapered sausages of palest blue modelling paste and stick in place, curving the paste over the top of each eye. Model a tiny teardrop shape from the same paste for the earring. Cut out the hair shape from brown modelling paste using the template and smooth the edge as before. Mark lines over the surface to add texture.

Gromit

10. Work on the cream cake on the green card. Using the template, cut out the top part of Gromit's face using palest brown modelling paste, smoothing the edge as before. For his muzzle, roll a ball with the remaining palest brown and press down to flatten slightly. Cut the side and bottom straight using the template as a cutting guide. Model eyes and a ball nose as before, and add a white highlight to each. Model his ears using brown modelling paste.

"How lovely - and unexpected."

Beware... the Were-rabbit!

The gigantic Were-rabbit is caught in the act of stealing the prize vegetables again and munching everything in his sight!

MATERIALS

20cm (8") and 15cm (6") square sponge cakes

625g (1lb 6oz) buttercream

Sugarpaste: 450g (1lb) dark brown, 1.44kg (3lb 2$\frac{1}{2}$oz) golden brown

Modelling paste: tiny piece of black, 30g (1oz) golden brown, 75g (2$\frac{1}{2}$oz) green, 10g ($\frac{1}{4}$oz) orange, 90g (3oz) pale green, 25g (just over $\frac{3}{4}$oz) palest pink, 10g ($\frac{1}{4}$oz) white

Paste food colours: brown and dark green (SK)

Icing sugar in a sugar shaker

Edible glue

A few drops of cooled, boiled water

2 sugar sticks

EQUIPMENT

30cm (12") round cake board

Large and small rolling pins

Pastry brush

Palette knife

Serrated carving knife

Straight-bladed cutting knife

Sable paintbrush: no. 2 (SK)

New, clean pan scourer

Recipes and a baking chart can be found on pages 8 to 15

METHOD

Covering the Board

1. Knead the dark brown sugarpaste until soft and pliable. Dampen the cake board with a little cooled, boiled water, roll out the sugarpaste on a non-stick board or work surface dusted with a sprinkling of icing sugar to prevent sticking and cover the cake board. Press the scourer over the surface to texture and then trim off any excess paste from around the edge. Set aside to dry.

Carving and Covering the Cake

2. Using a serrated knife, trim the crust from both cakes and level the tops. Cut the larger cake in two, making one piece a fraction larger than the other, and stack centrally together with the largest piece at the base. Cut the second cake in half exactly and

stack both pieces on top, making a total of four layers. To sculpt the body shape, trim off all four corners, cutting down and outwards from the top so the cake is wider at the bottom. Trim to round the shoulders and back, and then trim around the base to curve in slightly.

3. Sandwich all the layers together with buttercream. Spread buttercream on the underside and position on the cake board. Use the trimmings to shape the legs at the front, building up the cake for the knees and sandwiching the pieces together with buttercream. Spread a layer of buttercream over the cake to help the sugarpaste stick.

4. Roll out 900g (2lb) of golden brown sugarpaste. Sprinkle the surface with icing sugar and roll up into a spiral. Place the edge against the back of the cake and unroll the paste around the cake, trimming any excess paste away at the join. For the textured fur effect, press the scourer over the surface, pulling the scourer downwards occasionally to make the fur look longer in places.

5. For the arms, split 340g (12oz) of golden brown sugarpaste in half. Roll each half into a fat sausage shape and round off one end for the hand. Press the rounded end slightly flatter and make a cut for the thumb, no further than halfway. Make two more cuts across the top to separate fingers and pinch gently to round each finger off at the tip. Texture as before and then stick in position with a little edible glue, texturing further to disguise the joins.

6. To make the feet, split 90g (3oz) of golden brown sugarpaste in half and roll each piece into a long teardrop

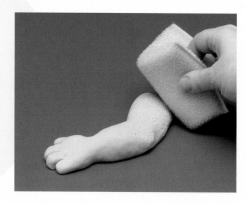

shape. Press down to flatten slightly, make two cuts into the fuller end of each one to separate the toes and round off the edges. Texture the top only and then stick the feet in position with 5g (just under 1/4oz) of golden brown sugarpaste pressed against the join. Texture the paste as before to disguise the join.

7. Model the head from 85g (2 3/4oz) of golden brown sugarpaste, following the step picture as a guide. Push the end of a paintbrush into the mouth area to open, turning up the corners slightly. Keep the indentation even so the teeth will sit straight. Indent the eye area and pinch the forehead upwards.

8. Thinly roll out some white modelling paste and cut a strip for the bottom teeth. Indent along the strip with the back of a knife to mark nine teeth. Model two small, square front teeth and two ball eyes with a black circular pupil on each. Using the remaining white modelling paste, model a ball-shaped tail. Make the nose with a small ball of palest pink modelling paste and indent nostrils with the end of a paintbrush.

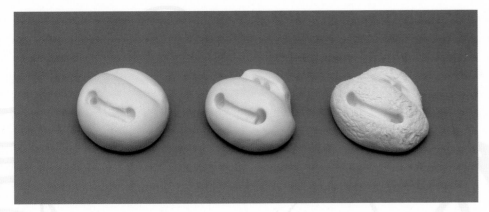

9. Stick the head onto the front of the cake with edible glue. Push some of the remaining golden brown sugarpaste into the join all around the head to help hold it securely and then disguise the join by texturing with the scourer. Push two sugar sticks into the top of the head to help support the ears later.

10. To make the footpads, split 10g (1/4oz) of palest pink modelling paste in half. Using one half, split again and roll one piece into an oval shape for the large pad on the heel. Make the three smaller toe pads using the second piece. Model the pads on the other foot in the same way.

11. To make the ears, split the golden brown modelling paste in half and roll into long teardrop shapes. Press a paintbrush handle into the centre to indent and roll gently at the wide end to open up the ear further. For the inner ears, split the remaining palest pink modelling paste in half and roll into long teardrop shapes. Press flat, and then stick into each ear. Texture the fur effect with the scourer as before. Push each ear gently onto a sugar stick to make a hole and then remove. Bend each ear forward slightly and set aside to dry.

Vegetables

12. To make the marrow, roll the pale green modelling paste into a fat teardrop shape and press into the centre to hollow out. Pinch up an edge and press into the surface with your finger to make bite marks. Indent the bottom of the marrow using the end of a paintbrush.

Smooth the ridges with your fingertips and then bend upwards slightly. For the striped effect, dilute some dark green paste food colour with a few drops of cooled, boiled water and paint stripes over the surface. Allow to dry before placing in position.

13. To make the carrots, split the orange modelling paste into different sized pieces and roll into long teardrop shapes. Mark the ridges by rolling a knife over the surface. Cut some to make them look half-eaten. For the carrot tops, roll long teardrops of green modelling paste and make feathery cuts down both sides. Dilute a little brown paste food colour with cooled, boiled water to make a translucent colour wash and paint a little over each carrot.

To Finish

14. Stick the ears in position over each sugar stick, securing with a little edible glue at the base and using some golden brown trimmings textured at the join as before.

"Beware!
Beware the beast within!"

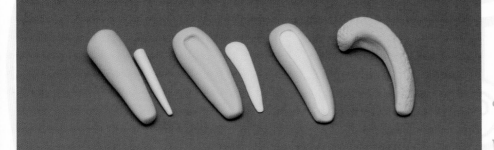

Knit One, Purl One

A familiar scene at 62 West Wallaby Street, Gromit sits comfortably in his very own armchair surrounded by 1950s inspired décor. When he's not keeping his beloved owner company, the ever-practical Gromit can even turn his paw to knitting.

Recipes and a baking chart can be found on pages 8 to 15

MATERIALS

25cm (10") square sponge cake

450g (1lb) buttercream

Sugarpaste: 400g (14oz) ivory, 800g (1lb 12oz) pale blue and 30g (1oz) yellow

Modelling paste: small ball of black, 175g (6oz) cream, 5g (just under $^1/_4$oz) dark blue, 145g (5oz) palest brown, 30g (1oz) pink and a small ball of white

Pastillage: 10g ($^1/_4$oz) brown and just under 5g ($^1/_8$oz) grey

Paste food colours: blue, brown, green, orange, red and yellow (SK)

Icing sugar in a sugar shaker

Edible glue

30-45ml (1-2tbsp) cooled, boiled water

Sugar stick

EQUIPMENT

30cm (12") round cake board

Large and small rolling pins

Pastry brush

Cake smoother

Palette knife

Serrated carving knife

Straight-bladed cutting knife

Sable paintbrushes: no. 1 and 2 (SK)

Paint palette

Bone or ball tool

Miniature circle cutter or no. 18 piping nozzle

New, clean pan scourer

Foam pieces (for support)

METHOD

Covering the Board

1. Knead the ivory sugarpaste until soft and pliable. Slightly dampen the cake board with a little cooled, boiled water, roll out the sugarpaste on a non-stick board or work surface dusted with a sprinkling of icing sugar to prevent sticking and cover the cake board. Make small cuts around the edge, creating the frilled rug effect.

2. Dilute some brown and orange paste food colours with cooled, boiled water to achieve a watercolour paint consistency and paint swirls and leaves over the surface of the covered board. Leave the paint to dry and then press the scourer gently over the surface to add texture. Set aside to dry completely.

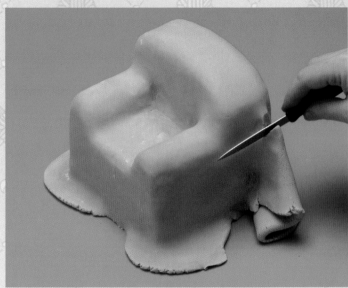

Carving and Covering the Cake

3. Trim the crust off the cake and level the top. For the base of the chair, cut an oblong from one side of the cake measuring 13cm x 15cm (5" x 6"). For the back of the chair, cut an oblong measuring 10cm x 15cm (4" x 6"). From the remaining cake, cut two chair arms measuring 4cm x 6cm (1^1/$_2$" x 2^1/$_2$") and an 8cm (3") square for the seat cushion. (The chair arms and seat cushion may have to be trimmed depending on how your cake has risen.) Trim half the depth from the seat cushion.

4. Cut a layer in the base cake. Place the back of the chair upright on top of the base cake, in line with the back of the base. Make sure that it is level and well balanced. Place the seat cushion and arms on top and trim if necessary. Trim a curve in the back piece and trim the top edge from each arm to round off. Trim either side of the armchair so the sides curve in slightly. Sandwich all layers and

parts together with buttercream, then spread a layer over the cake to help the sugarpaste stick.

5. Roll out the pale blue sugarpaste and cover the armchair completely, smoothing around the shape, stretching out any pleats and smoothing the paste downwards. Pull up the excess paste at the back corners and slice away, pressing the join closed and securing with a little edible glue. Rub the join closed with a little icing sugar on your fingers. Trim off any excess paste from around the base. Rub the surface gently with a cake smoother.

6. Spread a little buttercream onto the area on the cake board where the cake will sit. To reduce the possibility of marking the sugarpaste with your hands, quickly pick up the armchair cake, holding it at either side, and position on the cake board. Smooth a line under the seat cushion using your finger and press a dip in the seat ready for Gromit's body.

7. Thinly roll out the yellow sugarpaste and set aside for a few

moments, allowing the surface to dry out a little. Meanwhile, roll thin sausages for the piping along the front of the arms and across the back of the chair and secure in place. Using the miniature circle cutter (or no. 18 piping nozzle) cut 20-30 circles at a time from the rolled out paste. Pick each circle up individually using the brush dampened with edible glue and press onto the surface of the armchair covering.

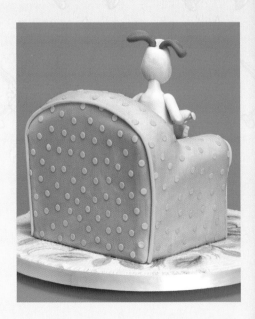

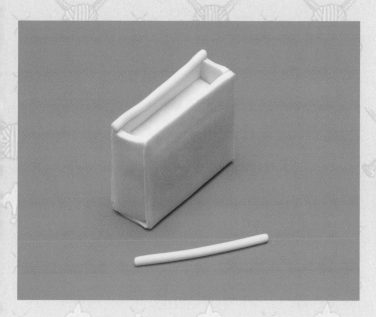

Knitting Bag and Cushion

8. Make the knitting needles next using the grey pastillage. Thinly roll out four slightly tapered sausage shapes and then roll out and cut four circles using the miniature circle cutter, pressing down onto each one to soften the cut edge. After a few moments the pastillage will set, so assemble the knitting needles with edible glue and set aside to dry.

9. To make the knitting bag supports and handles, roll the brown pastillage into a sausage and cut six lengths measuring 8cm (3"). Cut two exactly in half and shorten all the resulting four lengths slightly, allowing for the cross. Set all pieces aside to dry.

10. To make the cushion, roll 35g (1¼oz) of cream modelling paste into a ball, press down to flatten slightly and pinch four corners. Flatten around the edge and then roll the paintbrush over the surface of this flattened paste to thin and frill.

11. For the knitting bag, roll out 60g (2oz) of cream modelling paste and cut an oblong measuring 4cm x 6cm (1½" x 2½") for the inside of the bag. To cover the bag, thinly roll out 15g (½oz) of cream paste and cut two panels for the opposite ends, cutting both slightly higher than the top and trimming a slight curve so the fabric-effect covering looks like it has sagged a little. Roll out the remainder and cut an oblong to cover both sides and the bottom in one piece with the excess paste at the top. Stick this piece to the end panels with edible glue. Roll the trimmings into sausages to edge along the top on both sides of the bag.

12. To paint the detailing on the knitting bag and cushion, dilute red, blue, yellow and green paste food colours separately with cooled, boiled water to achieve a paint consistency. Paint the detailing, starting with the red flowers on the knitting bag using the no. 1 paintbrush. Paint blue around the red flowers and then paint yellow dots with faint red outlines. Paint roses and leaves on the cushion.

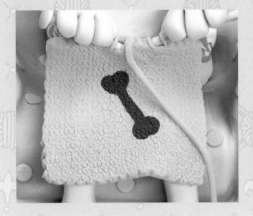

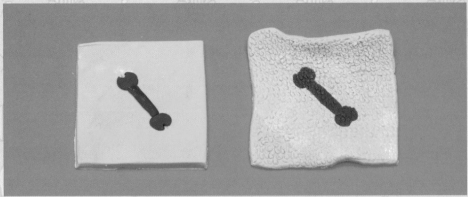

Gromit

13. To make Gromit's body, roll 60g (2oz) of palest brown modelling paste into a long teardrop shape and pinch gently at the narrow end to create a neck. Lay flat and press gently to flatten slightly and then stick centrally on the chair, making sure the figure is well balanced. Push a sugar stick down through the neck, leaving a little protruding to help hold the head in place later.

14. For the legs, split 25g (just over $^3/_4$oz) of palest brown paste in half and follow the instructions in the How to Model Wallace and Gromit section (see page 26). Stick the legs in place on the chair. Model Gromit's head using 30g (1oz) of palest brown, again following the instructions (see pages 25 to 26). Secure the head in place over the sugar stick.

15. For the knitting, roll out 20g ($^3/_4$oz) of pink modelling paste and cut a 5cm (2") square. For the bone, stick on a tiny strip of blue paste. Model two tiny flattened circles, indent each one using a cocktail stick and then stick in position at either end of the strip. Press the scourer firmly into the

surface to create a knitted texture. Stick this square of knitting onto Gromit's lap, turning it out at the top slightly. Stick two knitting needles into the top, pushing in just far enough to be held securely.

16. To make Gromit's arms, split the remaining palest brown modelling paste in half and follow the instructions on modelling (see page 26). Stick in position with his hands wrapped around the knitting needles. Take care not to break the needles with the weight of the hands; you may need to use foam pieces to support the hands until they are dry. Push the second pair of needles into the knitting bag.

To Finish

17. Make all the wool using the remaining pink and blue modelling paste. Roll a long, thin sausage of pink and stick on the centre of the knitting, curling the paste around and down to the cake board. Roll a sausage into a bundle and stick this onto the end. Roll tiny sausages and stick in place so that they are looped over the needles. Make balls of wool for the knitting bag by rolling paste into oval shapes and indenting the centre. Mark lines by rolling a knife over the surface.

18. When the brown pastillage pieces are dry, stick them in place on the knitting bag for the side supports and handles.

"Well, that went as well as could be expected, didn't it!"

Anyone for Football?

Wallace is a huge football fan and loves getting dressed in his full strip to have a kick around in the park with Gromit. The only trouble is, Gromit is somewhat more skilled than his owner, so Wallace reveals his latest invention – the Soccamatic!

MATERIALS

2 x 1 litre (2 pint) bowl-shaped sponge cakes

450g (1lb) buttercream

Sugarpaste: 340g (12oz) green and 650g (1lb 7oz) pale brown

Modelling paste: tiny ball of black, 20g ($^3/_4$oz) blue, 20g ($^3/_4$oz) flesh, 15g ($^1/_2$oz) golden brown and 30g (1oz) white

Icing sugar in a sugar shaker

Edible glue

A few drops of cooled, boiled water

1 sugar stick

EQUIPMENT

25cm (10") round cake board

Large and small rolling pins

Pastry brush

Cake smoother

Palette knife

Serrated carving knife

Straight-bladed cutting knife

Sable paintbrush: no. 2 (SK)

Ball or bone tool

New, clean pan scourer

A few cocktail sticks

Foam sheet or kitchen paper

Foam pieces (for support)

Template (see page 123)

Recipes and a baking chart can be found on pages 8 to 15

METHOD
Preparing the Board and Cake

1. Knead the green sugarpaste until soft and pliable. Slightly dampen the cake board with a little cooled, boiled water, roll out the sugarpaste on a non-stick board or work surface dusted with a sprinkling of icing sugar to prevent sticking and cover the cake board. Texture the surface by pressing in firmly with the scourer. Trim off any excess paste from around the edge and then set aside to dry.

2. Trim the crust from each cake and level the tops. Put the two cakes together and check they make a perfect ball shape. If the shape is elongated, trim further to make it more rounded. Sandwich the two cakes together, then spread a layer of buttercream over the surface to help the sugarpaste stick. Make sure that the buttercream completely covers the whole cake and then put the cake aside to allow the surface of the buttercream to firm (this helps when covering the cake later).

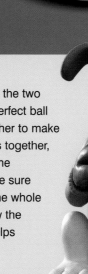

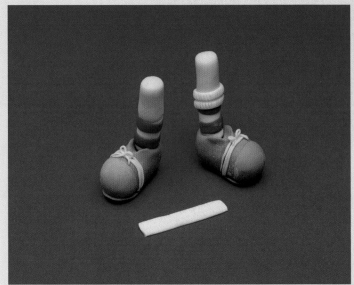

Wallace

3. Set aside one third of the golden brown modelling paste. To make Wallace's football boots, split the remainder in half and roll one piece into an oval shape. Push into one end using the end of a paintbrush to open up the top of the boot, winding the brush around to open up the paste further. Indent the boot at the front using a cocktail stick and then pinch around the top of this opening, creating an edge. Make the second boot in the same way using the other half of the golden brown paste.

4. Using pea-sized amounts of golden brown modelling paste, roll two oval shapes and press flat. Stick one in place over the top of each boot at the toe area and smooth down and around the shape, keeping the join showing on the top. To make the soles, first set aside a tiny piece of golden brown modelling paste for the buttons later, and then split the remainder in half. Roll each piece into a sausage, roll the paste thinner just below halfway to make an indent and round off the lower end for the heel. Press each piece flat then smooth the top of both soles to spread out the paste slightly. Stick in place on the bottom of each boot.

5. For the laces, roll six very thin sausages of white modelling paste and stick three each over the top of each boot, tucking any excess underneath. For the ties, roll two more thin sausages, loop twice in the centre and then stick in place.

6. To make the football socks, split 5g (just under $^1/_4$oz) of white modelling paste in half and roll into sausages measuring 2cm ($^3/_4$"). Very thinly roll out a little blue modelling paste and

cut two strips for each sock. Wrap each strip around the front of the leg, keeping the join at the back. Stick the socks into the boots.

7. Split just under 5g ($^1/_8$oz) of flesh modelling paste in half and roll into sausages measuring 2cm ($^3/_4$") for legs. Stick these in place on top of each sock. To hold these pieces together securely, make sock tops by rolling two small sausages of white, press flat and then mark ribbing over the surface using a knife. Indent down the centre of each using a paintbrush handle to create a pleat and then stick in place, wrapping the

paste around the join between the sock and the leg.

8. Make Wallace's shorts next using 15g (1/2oz) of blue modelling paste. Roll the paste into a ball and press down onto the top to flatten slightly. Make a cut at the bottom to separate the legs. Pinch around the edge of each leg to create a ridge. Squeeze either side of the shorts to narrow the paste and press down on the waistband area. Mark fabric effect pleats with a cocktail stick. Lay the shorts down flat and stick the legs in position. From this point, Wallace is built up laying flat and left to dry completely before he is positioned on the cake.

9. To make Wallace's football shirt, roll 15g (1/2oz) of white modelling paste into a teardrop shape and press down on the point to flatten for his neck area. Pinch around the full end to create an edge and hollow out slightly to make room for the shorts. Lay the shirt flat, stroke the sides to straighten and then press down to flatten slightly. Thinly roll out some blue modelling paste and cut

out three strips. Stick each one in place on the shirt with one small strip covering the top and two wrapped around the front of the shirt. Join neatly at the back. Push a sugar stick into the neck to support the head later.

10. For the sleeves, split just under 5g (1/4oz) of white modelling paste in half and model two teardrop shapes. Using the end of a paintbrush, hollow out the full end of each to make room for the arm to slot in. Stick the sleeves in place and then add one blue stripe on each. Split 10g (1/4oz) of flesh modelling paste in half and make the arms, following the instructions in the How to Model Wallace and Gromit section (see page 25). Once you have made the arms, cut off the top of each one to allow for the sleeve length, and then stick each arm securely into each sleeve. Put a little piece of foam sponge behind the waving arm to bring it forward slightly and allow to firm in this position.

11. Using the remaining flesh modelling paste, make Wallace's head following the instructions in the How to Model Wallace and Gromit section (see page 24). Push the head gently onto the sugar stick, securing at the base with edible glue. You may need to place a small piece of foam sponge at the back of the head for extra support. Thinly roll out a little white modelling paste and cut a small strip for the collar. Model three tiny golden brown buttons for the yoke. Thinly roll out the white trimmings and cut out the shirt badge. Stick these final details in position with edible glue.

Covering the Football

12. When the surface of the buttercream on the cake has set firmly, it is ready for the covering to be applied. Spread a little more buttercream over the surface so the sugarpaste will stick easily or rework the surface with a palette knife that has been dipped in warm, boiled water.

13. Prepare the template on greaseproof paper: you may need to adjust the shape slightly to allow for the shape of your cake, as no two cakes are ever exactly the same. To cover the cake, roll out some pale brown sugarpaste and cut one shape. Stick this shape onto the bottom of the cake and smooth gently over the surface, using a cake smoother if required. This smoothing action may stretch the surface, making the lines uneven, so re-trim if necessary. Position the cake centrally on the cake board, with the covered part on the base, and secure with a little edible glue.

14. Cut out another shape and cover the top of the cake. Complete the covering with four more shapes, covering the front and back first, then either side. Press the joins closed without losing the join lines. Mark two lines over each shape using a knife. Using the sugarpaste trimmings, cut six small strips for the lacing and stick in place down the front of the football.

To Finish

15. When Wallace's figure is dry, stick him in position with edible glue, resting against the football for support. Ensure the figure is well balanced to achieve a natural look.

"Oh, now that's just not cricket, Gromit!"

Through the Porthole!

This classic image of Wallace and Gromit peeking out of the rocket's porthole window is both fun and familiar and works perfectly as a celebration cake.

MATERIALS

25cm (10") round sponge cake

450g (1lb) buttercream

Sugarpaste: 900g (2lb) pale green

Modelling paste: 5g (just under $^1/_4$oz) black, 20g ($^3/_4$oz) brown, 10g ($^1/_4$oz) dark green, 125g (4$^1/_2$oz) flesh, 450g (1lb) orange, 145g (5oz) palest brown, small ball of red, 20g ($^3/_4$oz) white

Icing sugar in a sugar shaker

Edible glue

EQUIPMENT

25cm (10") round cake board

30cm (12") and 20cm (8") round cake cards or plates (to cut around)

Large and small rolling pins

Palette knife

Serrated carving knife

Straight-bladed cutting knife

Sable paintbrush: no. 2 (SK)

Ball or bone tool

A few cocktail sticks

Recipes and a baking chart can be found on pages 8 to 15

METHOD

Carving and Covering the Cake

1. Trim the crust from the cake and level the top. Cut two layers in the cake and then sandwich the layers together with buttercream. Spread buttercream on the underside of the cake and position on the cake board. Spread a layer of buttercream over the surface to help the sugarpaste stick.

2. To achieve a straight and supportive edge for the porthole edging, cover the top and sides of the cake separately. Knead 500g (1lb 1$^3/_4$oz) of pale green sugarpaste until soft and pliable and then roll out on a non-stick board or work surface dusted with a sprinkling of icing sugar to prevent sticking. Cover the top of the cake only, and then trim the edge neatly.

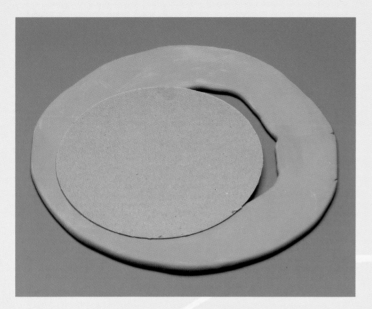

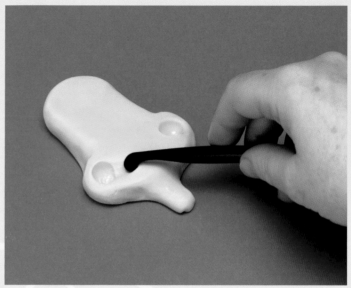

3. Roll out the remaining pale green sugarpaste, including trimmings from the top of the cake, and cut a strip the height of the cake and measuring at least 80cm (32") in length. Sprinkle this strip with icing sugar to prevent sticking and then roll in to a spiral. Place against the side of the cake and unroll the paste around it, trimming off the excess paste from the join. Secure with a little edible glue and smooth over the join with icing sugar on your fingers to remove the line completely. This covering should be level with the edge of the cake board.

4. For the porthole, roll the orange modelling paste into a sausage and loop this round into a circle. Firmly press the join closed and then roll out further, stretching the paste until the centre is slightly less than 20cm (8") in diameter. Place the 20cm (8") cake card or plate down onto it and cut around the edge to make a neat circle. Smooth this cut line to soften the edge. Repeat with the 30cm (12") card or plate to make a neat ring.

5. Model eight ball-shaped bolts using the orange trimmings and stick in place using edible glue. Set the porthole aside to dry, making sure that it is completely circular. As a guide for where to position the figures, place the 20cm (8") card or plate centrally on top of the cake and score around the outside edge using a cocktail stick.

Wallace

6. To make Wallace's head, roll 115g (4oz) of flesh modelling paste into a fat sausage and round off one end. Press down onto the work surface to flatten. Pinch gently at the bottom of the rounded end to bring down Wallace's neck. Push a ball or bone tool either side to indent the corners of the mouth and then smooth the paste in-between to open it up into a smile. Smooth a neat ridge for the bottom lip. Stroke gently either side of the mouth at the top to define the lips.

7. Smooth the top of Wallace's head and pinch up slightly at the forehead, smoothing out any marks. Indent two eye sockets side by side using the ball or bone tool. Stick on a flattened

ball for the nose. To make the ears, roll two small ball shapes of flesh modelling paste and indent the centre of each using the ball or bone tool. Cut a little paste from the side of each and then press at the top and bottom and the outside edge to make the ears slightly angular.

8. For Wallace's teeth, thinly roll out some white modelling paste and cut a strip. Indent the strip with the back of a knife to mark teeth. Indent eight for the bottom set and four slightly wider teeth for the top. Secure in place with edible glue. Roll two ball-shaped eyes and stick on a flattened circle of black modelling paste for each pupil.

9. To make Wallace's shirt, split 5g (just under $^1/_4$oz) of white modelling paste in half. Roll one half into a teardrop shape and press flat. Position Wallace's head on the cake and then stick the shirt in position at the bottom of Wallace's neck, following the marked outline of the porthole as a guide.

10. For the pullover, split the dark green modelling paste into six equal pieces. Roll each piece into a

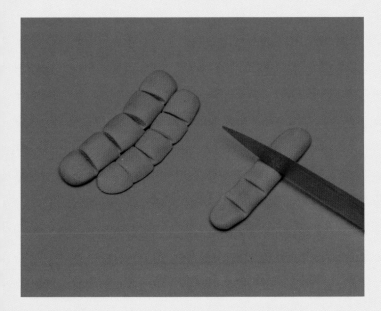

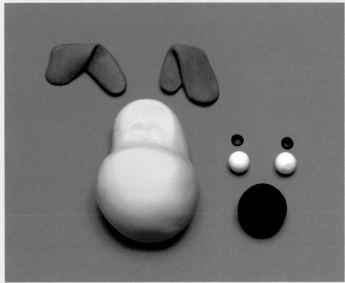

sausage and press down to flatten slightly. Mark indentations with a knife and press again to round off. Stick the paste in strips around Wallace's shirt, building up the knitted effect.

11. Stick two small, flattened pieces of white modelling paste either side of the green for shoulders. Roll two tiny pea-sized balls of white modelling paste into teardrop shapes, press flat and use for the collar on either side. Model the tie from red paste by making a tapered sausage and a small teardrop for the knot.

Gromit

12. For Gromit's body, flatten 20g (³/₄oz) of palest brown modelling paste into an oval shape and stick widthways on the cake. Smooth down the paste following the marked outline. Indent a line for an arm and smooth with your fingertip.

13. To make his head, roll a ball using 100g (3¹/₂oz) of palest brown modelling paste. Press just above halfway for the eye area and then pinch out the forehead, smoothing to remove any marks. Round off the muzzle by stroking gently over the shape. Indent the eye sockets side by side using the ball or bone tool. Secure the head to the cake using edible glue.

14. Stick on eyes as before and roll the remaining black modelling paste into a ball for his nose. Split the brown modelling paste in half and model two teardrop-shaped ears. Fold each ear over and stick in position with a little edible glue.

With the remaining flesh modelling paste, model part of Wallace's hand resting on Gromit's shoulder.

15. When the porthole edging is dry, stick this in position on the cake. Split the remaining palest brown modelling paste in half and use this to make Gromit's hands. Roll into oval shapes and make cuts to separate a thumb on opposite sides and two cuts along the top of each to separate three fingers. Press down to flatten slightly and smooth out the fingertips to round off. Stick in position resting on the edge of the porthole.

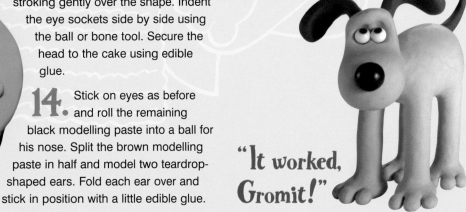

"It worked, Gromit!"

Bunnies Everywhere

There was the cutest little production line of bunnies when I was making this cake! The shapes required to build them up are very simple so you'll be able to create them easily. If time is short, make their heads only and position them onto the larger spots decorating the cake.

MATERIALS

13cm (5") and 20cm (8") round sponge cakes

625g (1lb 6oz) buttercream

Sugarpaste: 550g (1lb 3^1/$_2$oz) lilac, 1.3kg (2lb 13^3/$_4$oz) pink, 60g (2oz) pale lilac and 60g (2oz) white

Modelling paste: 5g (just under ^{1}/$_4$oz) black, 130g (4^1/$_2$oz) brown, 130g (4^1/$_2$oz) grey, 130g (4^1/$_2$oz) cream, tiny ball of green, 15g (^{1}/$_2$oz) pale pink, 15g (^{1}/$_2$oz) white and tiny ball of yellow

Icing sugar in a sugar shaker

Edible glue

A few drops of cooled, boiled water

13 sugar sticks

EQUIPMENT

35cm (14") round cake board

13cm (5") round cake card

Large and small rolling pins

Pastry brush

Cake smoother

Palette knife

Serrated carving knife

Straight-bladed cutting knife

3 food-grade plastic dowels

Sable paintbrush: no. 1 (SK)

1.5cm (^{1}/$_2$"), 2cm (^{3}/$_4$") and 2.5cm (1") circle cutters

Pencil

Bone or ball tool

Plain piping nozzle: no. 3

A few cocktail sticks

Recipes and a baking chart can be found on pages 8 to 15

METHOD

Covering the Cake and Board

1. Knead 500g (1lb 1^3/$_4$oz) of lilac sugarpaste until soft and pliable. Slightly dampen the cake board with a little cooled, boiled water, roll out the sugarpaste on a non-stick board or work surface dusted with a sprinkling of icing sugar to prevent sticking and cover the cake board. Rub over the surface with a cake smoother and then trim off any excess paste from around the edge. Cut out different sized circles around the edge of the cake board using the circle cutters and then set aside to dry.

2. Using a serrated knife, trim the crust from both cakes and level each cake top. Cut two layers in each cake and sandwich back together with buttercream. Spread buttercream on the underside of each cake. Place the larger cake on the centre of the cake board and the smaller cake on the cake card. Cover the surface of both cakes with a thin layer of buttercream to help the sugarpaste stick.

3. Roll out 900g (2lb) of pink sugarpaste and cover the large cake completely, smoothing down and around the shape to expel any air. Trim away the excess paste from around the base. Rub the surface with the cake smoother and then trim around the base again to obtain a neat edging.

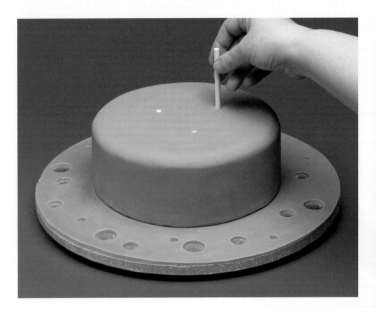

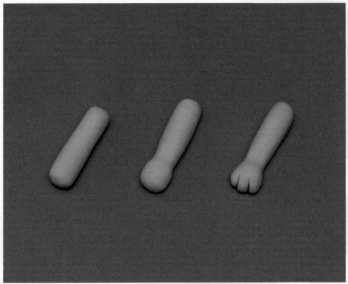

4. To help support the top cake, push all three dowelling rods down into the large cake, spacing them evenly and no more than 5cm (2") from the centre. Using a pencil, mark each dowelling rod level with the top of the cake (ensure the pencil does not come into contact with the sugarpaste). Remove the dowels, place them side-by-side on a flat surface and mark again using a knife, cutting into the plastic only slightly using the highest mark of all three. Snap the dowelling rods at the cut mark so that they are all the required length. Push the dowelling rods back into the holes in the cake until they are level with the surface.

5. Roll out the remaining pink sugarpaste, cover the smaller cake as before and then position the cake (with cake card) centrally on top of the larger cake. Cut out and remove circles of sugarpaste as before from around the cake sides.

6. Roll out the lilac, pale lilac, pink and white sugarpaste one at a time and cut out circles to fill the holes on the board and cake. Smooth over the join with your finger.

Bunnies

Note: You will need to make thirteen bunnies altogether, six to go around each cake and one on the top. Start by making one each out of the brown, grey and cream modelling paste, and then knead the remaining colours together in different quantities to make different shades of brown and grey.

7. To make a bunny, make the body first by rolling 15g (1/2oz) of modelling paste into a teardrop shape. Pinch gently around the centre to indent the paste and press on the top to flatten.

8. For the arms, split 5g (just under 1/4oz) into four equally sized pieces. Roll two into sausage shapes, slightly rounding off the end of each for the paws. Indent each paw twice with the back of a knife. Stick the arms in place with a little edible glue, smooth the joins closed with your fingers and rub gently with a little icing sugar to blend completely. Roll the other two pieces into teardrop shapes for feet and mark the paws in the same way as before.

9. Push a sugar stick down through the body, leaving a little protruding at the top to help hold the head in place. Roll 5g (just under 1/4oz) of modelling paste into a ball for the head and then pinch gently at the eye area to flatten. Stick two pea-sized amounts either side for cheeks, blending in the join using a no. 1 sable paintbrush with a little edible glue. Smooth the surface with icing sugar on your fingertips.

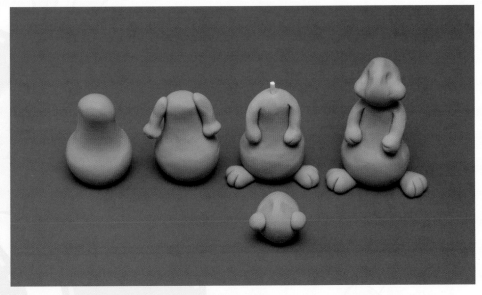

10. To indent the eye sockets, push the small end of a bone or ball tool into the eye area. For the muzzle, roll a pea-sized amount of pale pink modelling paste into an oval shape and press flat. Stick in place and mark two nostrils with the tip of a cocktail stick. Using white modelling paste, roll two tiny balls for the eyes, cut a tiny square for the front teeth and mark down the centre with the back of a knife, and model a ball-shaped tail, pinching the surface to add texture.

11. For the ears, roll two small teardrop shapes 2cm ($^3/_4$") in length. Roll the end of a paintbrush into the centre to indent the paste and push up the paste around the edge. Roll two long teardrops of pale pink paste and smooth gently into the recess in each ear. Make small holes in the top of the head using the end of a paintbrush and stick the ears in place with edible glue, holding for a few moments until they are secure.

12. Roll out a little black modelling paste and cut out the eyes using a no. 3 plain piping nozzle. Press down on each circle to flatten the cut edge and secure in place.

13. To make the daisy in the top bunny's mouth, roll out and cut a circle of white modelling paste using the smallest circle cutter. Make small cuts all around the outside edge and then indent the centre using the bone or ball tool. Stick a flattened circle of yellow paste in the centre and texture this using the tip of a cocktail stick. Roll a tiny thin sausage of green paste for the stalk. Secure the daisy in place with a little edible glue.

"That's just grand."

Train Chase

One of the most famous scenes from The Wrong Trousers is the train chase, when between them, Wallace and Gromit manage to capture the villain, 'Feathers' McGraw. This high-speed adventure is a great theme for a celebration cake.

MATERIALS

20cm (8") round sponge cake

450g (1lb) buttercream

Sugarpaste: 1.25kg (2lb 12oz) white

Modelling paste: 315g (11oz) black, 30g (1oz) blue, 10g ($^1/_4$oz) brown, 10g ($^1/_4$oz) golden brown, 160g (5$^1/_2$oz) flesh, 60g (2oz) grey, small piece of orange, 135g (4$^3/_4$oz) palest brown, 175g (6oz) red and 60g (2oz) white

Pastillage: 5g (just under $^1/_4$oz) white

Paste food colour: brown (SK)

Metallic lustre dust food colours: gold and silver (SK)

Icing sugar in a sugar shaker

Edible glue

A few drops of cooled, boiled water

5ml (1tsp) clear alcohol (e.g. vodka or gin)

3 sugar sticks

EQUIPMENT

35cm (14") round cake board

Large and small rolling pins

Pastry brush

Cake smoother

Palette knife

Serrated carving knife

Straight-bladed cutting knife

Sable paintbrushes: nos. 1 and 2

Miniature square cutter

Ball or bone tool

New, clean pan scourer

Piping nozzles: nos. 3, 4, 17 and 18

A few cocktail sticks

Foam sponge pieces (for support)

Recipes and a baking chart can be found on pages 8 to 15

METHOD

Covering the Cake and Board

1. Knead 500g (1lb 1$^3/_4$oz) of white sugarpaste until soft and pliable. Slightly dampen the cake board with a little cooled, boiled water, roll out the sugarpaste on a non-stick board or work surface dusted with a sprinkling of icing sugar to prevent sticking and cover the cake board. Rub over the surface with a cake smoother and then trim off any excess paste from around the edge. Set aside to dry.

2. Using a serrated knife, trim the crust from the cake and level the top. Cut two layers in the cake and sandwich back together with buttercream. Spread buttercream on the underside of the cake and position centrally on the cake board. Cover the surface with a thin layer of buttercream to help the sugarpaste stick.

3. Roll out the remaining white sugarpaste and cover the cake completely, smoothing down and around the shape to expel any air. Trim away the excess paste from around the base. Rub the surface with the cake smoother and then trim around the base again to obtain a neat edging. Mark lines to indicate the speeding train around the cake and cake board by indenting with the end of a paintbrush.

4. Thinly roll out the black modelling paste and cut several thin strips at a time measuring 5cm (2") in length for the train tracks. Stick these in position around the cake board using edible glue. Thinly roll out the grey modelling paste and cut strips around 15-20cm (6-8") in length for the rails. Lay the strips in place and close the joins by using a little edible glue and rubbing gently.

Net

5. To allow for drying time, make the net next. Roll 5g (just under $^1/_4$oz) pastillage into a long, thin sausage for the handle and lay flat. Dilute a little brown paste food colour with a few drops of cooled, boiled water to achieve a watercolour paint consistency and paint the net handle, leaving streaks to resemble a wood effect. For the net, roll out 35g (1$^1/_4$oz) of black modelling paste and cut a 9cm (3$^1/_2$") triangle. Cut out circles by pressing repeatedly over the surface using the no. 3 nozzle and then loop the paste round and stick two sides

together. Push a piece of foam into the top to hold it open and set aside to dry.

Train

6. Make the base of the engine by thickly rolling out 30g (1oz) of black modelling paste and cutting an oblong shape measuring 2.5cm x 5.5cm (1" x 2 $^1/_4$"). Roll out a further 60g (2oz) of black paste and cut five slightly thinner bases for the carriages measuring 1.5cm x 6cm ($^1/_2$" x 2$^1/_4$"). For the trolley Wallace is sitting on, cut another black oblong slightly smaller than one of the carriage bases and stick this onto the bottom. Cut a 2.5cm (1") square for the blue engine fuel trolley.

7. Roll 5g (just under $^1/_4$oz) of blue modelling paste into a sausage and cut both ends straight. Stick centrally on top of the base. Roll out a further 15g ($^1/_2$oz) of blue paste and cut a square and two small oblongs for the engine cab, then cut a small semi-circle from each side using the no. 18 nozzle. Roll out a

tiny piece of grey modelling paste and cut two strips for the engine, one slightly thicker for the bumper. Cut out two circles from the grey with the no. 4 nozzle and indent in the centre with the no. 3 nozzle. Roll out 10g ($^1/_4$oz) of blue paste and cut the four sides for the engine fuel trolley.

8. Using 10g ($^1/_4$oz) of black modelling paste, make the front of the engine, funnel, circular bumpers (using the no. 17 piping nozzle) and cut a square roof for the top of the cab. Roll out more black paste and cut 24 wheels using the 1cm ($^3/_8$") circle cutter. Indent each wheel with the no. 18 nozzle, mark lines using a knife and indent each centre using a cocktail stick.

9. Make four more slightly larger wheels for the engine by shaping circles and indenting into the centre as before using the 1cm ($^3/_8$") circle cutter. Colour the surface of each wheel with a little silver metallic dust food colour on your fingertips. Stick the wheels in position against the blue engine and add the grey wheel supports.

10. Thickly roll out the red modelling paste, cut four oblong carriages measuring 2cm x 5cm ($^3/_4$" x 2") and stick one onto each base. Thinly roll out some black modelling paste and cut forty windows using the miniature square cutter. Stick five windows on each side using edible glue. Thinly roll out some grey modelling paste and cut oblong roofs for each carriage measuring 2.5cm x 6cm (1 x 2$^1/_2$"). Stick the wheels in position.

11. Mix some gold metallic dust food colour with a few drops of clear alcohol to achieve a paint consistency. Using the no. 1 paintbrush, paint the lines decorating the engine and carriages. Assemble the engine and carriages on the track around the cake board, securing with a little edible glue.

'Feathers' McGraw

12. Roll 30g (1oz) of black modelling paste into a teardrop and pinch gently around the top to narrow the neck and round off the head. Roll a small ball of white modelling paste into a teardrop shape, press flat and stick onto the front for the patch. To make the sack, first set aside a pea-sized amount of golden brown modelling paste and then roll the remainder into a teardrop. Push into the narrow end to open up the paste and pinch little pleats, gathering them and pressing them closed. Texture the surface with the scourer.

13. Split 5g (just under $^1/_4$oz) of black modelling paste in half and make his wings. Stick them in position against his body with

one outstretched and the other wrapped around and holding the sack. Model a teardrop-shaped beak using the orange modelling paste and add two tiny black eyes.

14. To make the gun, roll a small ball of grey modelling paste into a long, tapered sausage and bend halfway. Roll and straighten the narrow end and press down on the wider end to flatten the handle of the gun, cutting it straight at the bottom. To complete the gun, thinly roll out the black trimmings and cut a strip to edge the tip, loop little sausages round for the triggers and shape a barrel, indenting the surface with a cocktail stick.

15. Mix some silver dust food colour with a little clear alcohol and paint over the surface of the gun. Model a tiny teardrop with the golden brown paste reserved earlier, press it flat and stick in place on the handle of the gun. When the gun is dry, stick it in place against the wing, using foam pieces for support until dry.

Gromit

16. Model Gromit's body, arms, legs and head following the instructions in the How to Model Wallace and Gromit section (see pages 25 to 26). Use 65g (2^1/$_4$oz) of palest brown modelling paste for his body, 10g (^{1}/$_4$oz) each for the arms and legs, and the remainder for his head. Build up his figure on top of a carriage, securing the joins between his limbs closed with a little edible glue. To remove the join completely, stoke the paste gently and rub the surface with a little icing sugar on your fingers.

17. Push a sugar stick into the neck to help hold the head in position and wedge a foam piece underneath his muzzle for support until the head and body are completely dry. Model a pointed tail and use a sugar stick to hold it in position.

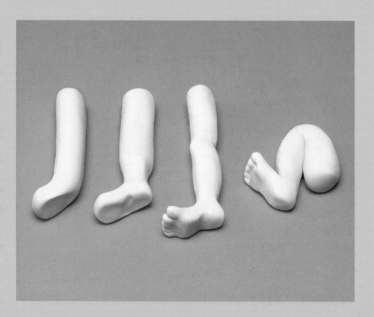

Wallace

18. To make Wallace's legs, split just under 60g (2oz) of flesh modelling paste in half. Roll one piece into a sausage and bend one end round for the foot. Pinch out a heel at the back. Squeeze gently at either side to narrow the foot and push up the underside of the foot to create the arch. Cut the toes and round off each one by smoothing the surface with your fingers. Bend the leg halfway, pinch out a knee and stick in position on the trolley with the foot resting on a carriage. Repeat for the second leg.

19. For Wallace's boxer shorts, roll 45g (1¼oz) of white modelling paste into a ball and pinch the top to open up the paste and create an edge for the waistband. Press down to flatten slightly and make a small cut in the bottom to separate the legs. Pinch the paste around each leg and then stick the shorts in position. Thinly roll out the red trimmings and cut out circles for the dots using the no. 4 piping nozzle. Stick the

dots in place over the boxers and pressing them gently into the surface to inlay the pattern.

20. For Wallace's body, roll 35g (1¼oz) of flesh modelling paste into an oval shape and pinch gently at the top for the neck. For the arms, split 35g (1¼oz) of flesh paste in half and follow the instructions in the How to Model Wallace and Gromit section (see page 25). Stick the arms on either side of the body and then stick the body in position, supported by the side of the cake and holding the net handle. Use foam pieces for support if necessary. Push a sugar stick down into the neck until a little is protruding to help support the head later.

21. Make Wallace's head next using the remaining flesh modelling paste, following the modelling instructions (see page 24). When making the mouth area, stick in a tiny flattened piece of red paste for the tongue.

22. For Wallace's vest, thinly roll out the remaining white modelling paste and cut two rectangles for the front and back. Cut out semi-circles for the

armholes and a neckline at the front. Repeatedly press the no. 3 piping tube over the surface to cut out holes and then stick both pieces in position on the body. Stick the net onto the handle, using a foam piece for support until dry.

"Most definitely not legal, this."

Gromit's Christmas Kennel

Here's Gromit checking out his full stocking from Santa. This design is a sweet and charming alternative to the usual Christmas cake, perfect for Gromit fans everywhere.

MATERIALS

30cm (12") square sponge cake

450g (1lb) buttercream

Sugarpaste: 800g (1lb 12oz) pale brown and 650g (1lb 7oz) white

Modelling paste: 30g (1oz) black, 10g ($^1/_4$oz) brown, 45g (1$^1/_2$oz) dark green, 120g (4$^1/_4$oz) palest brown, 75g (2$^1/_2$oz) red, 30g (1oz) white and 10g ($^1/_4$oz) yellow

Paste food colours: black and brown (SK)

Icing sugar in a sugar shaker

Edible glue

30-45ml (2-3tbsp) cooled, boiled water

EQUIPMENT

30cm (12") petal-shaped cake board

Large and small rolling pins

Pastry brush

Cake smoother

Palette knife

Serrated carving knife

Straight-bladed cutting knife

Sable paintbrushes: nos. 2 and 6

Large blossom cutter

Medium star cutter

New, clean pan scourer

Kitchen paper

Ruler

Recipes and a baking chart can be found on pages 8 to 15

METHOD

Carving and Covering the Cake

1. Trim the crust from the cake and slice the top flat. Cut the cake into four equal squares by cutting in half and then half again. Stack the cakes one on top of the other and trim one side so the cake is slightly oblong in shape. Cut down from the top layer on both sides to shape the pointed roof, taking off the top edge from the second layer of cake.

2. Spread buttercream on the underside of the bottom layer of cake and place it centrally on the cake board. Sandwich all layers together with buttercream then spread a layer over the surface of the cake to help the sugarpaste stick.

3. Measure the back of the cake, reducing the width measurement slightly to allow for the indented lines. Roll out 145g (5oz) of pale brown sugarpaste and cut a piece to cover the back of the cake. Indent lines evenly into the surface using a ruler and

mark a wood grain pattern using a sharp knife. Lift the sugarpaste carefully and press in place using a cake smoother.

4. Following the same method, cover the sides up to the roof level using 125g (4^1/$_2$oz) of sugarpaste for each, and then cover the front. Cut out an arched doorway in the front, ensuring the top reaches halfway up, and remove the sugarpaste. Thinly roll out 20g (3/4oz) of black modelling paste and cover this area, using the pale brown arch as a template.

5. Measure the top of the cake, roll out the remaining pale brown sugarpaste and cut a piece for the roof, slightly larger than the measurement. Carefully lift the paste and cover the top of the cake, then press a cake smoother along the edges to straighten them up.

6. Dilute some brown paste food colour with a little cooled, water to achieve a watercolour paint consistency. Using the no. 6 paintbrush, paint the kennel to create a wood effect. The sugarpaste may resist the colour at first, so keep brushing over the surface

until the sugar starts to dissolve slightly and then brush in the direction of the wood grain.

Decorations

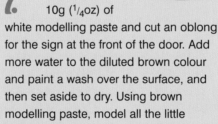

7. Thinly roll out 10g (^{1}/$_4$oz) of white modelling paste and cut an oblong for the sign at the front of the door. Add more water to the diluted brown colour and paint a wash over the surface, and then set aside to dry. Using brown modelling paste, model all the little flattened circles for the nail heads, sticking one next to the sign for the stocking handle.

8. Make the Christmas stocking using 65g (2^1/$_4$oz) of red modelling paste. Roll into a sausage and bend one end round for the foot. Pinch the paste to create an opening around the top. Thinly roll out 15g (^{1}/$_2$oz) of dark green modelling paste and cut strips to go around the stocking, then stick on a circle at the toe area. Press a sheet of kitchen paper over the surface for a fabric effect

(this will also inlay the stripes) and then set aside to dry.

9. Thinly roll out 200g (7oz) of white sugarpaste for the snowy roof covering and cut out a piece for the roof to the same measurement as before. Texture the surface with the scourer; this will flatten the paste, making it slightly larger so the snow falls just over the edge of the roof. Lift the paste and cover over the roof, then push gently along the edge with the scourer to texture further and create an uneven edge.

10. Thickly roll out the remaining white sugarpaste into a strip and press the rolling pin firmly into the paste to indent the surface. Wrap the strip around the base of the kennel, pressing your hands down onto the paste to create an uneven surface. Texture as before and trim away the excess paste from around the base.

11. Thinly roll out a little of the palest brown modelling paste and cut out a star. Set aside to dry. Stick the stocking in position with edible glue, then model a little red strip for the handle and loop it around the nail head.

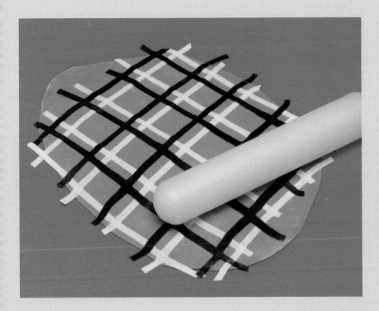

Gromit

12. To make Gromit's head and arms, use 90g (3oz) of palest brown modelling paste for his head and split the remainder in half for his two arms. Follow the instructions in the How to Model Wallace and Gromit section (see pages 25 to 26). Pinch up the forehead slightly more and push down on one side to give his face more expression.

13. For the tartan blanket, roll out 5g (just under $^1/_4$oz) each of yellow and black modelling paste as thinly as possible and cut into strips. Thinly roll out 20g ($^3/_4$oz) of dark green and, using a minimal amount of edible glue, stick the strips over the surface in a tartan pattern. Press gently with a cake smoother and then roll over the surface with the rolling pin to inlay the pattern. Cut out two squares, gather up the paste and stick in place over the top of each arm.

14. For the earmuffs, roll a sausage of black modelling paste and press to flatten slightly. Split 5g (just under $^1/_4$oz) of red modelling paste in half

and roll two ball shapes. Press the scourer into the surface to texture then stick in position.

To Finish

15. Using the remaining white modelling paste, make all the different sized bone tops. Roll a sausage and round off one end. Press the rounded end to flatten slightly and then indent with the back of a knife. Texture a tiny trimming of white modelling paste and stick this on the top surface of the star. Stick the star onto the roof with edible glue.

16. For the Christmas lights, roll very thin sausages of black modelling paste and loop them around the doorway. Cut blossom shapes using red, yellow and green modelling paste. Indent the centre of each and fill with a small ball of paste. Stick the lights in position at the top of each loop.

17. Dilute some black paste food colour with a few drops of cooled, boiled water and paint the wording on the sign using the no. 2 paintbrush. Stick the sign above the kennel door using edible glue, holding for a few moments until secure.

"Ho, ho, ho!"

Paw Print Cupcakes

If you're planning a party and looking for ideas, this project is quick and easy. Cupcakes are always extremely popular and you can decorate them with these fun and colourful paw prints inspired by Gromit.

MATERIALS

10-12 sponge cupcakes

Sugarpaste: 15g (¹/₂oz) white and 5g (just under ¹/₄oz) different coloured sugarpaste for each cupcake

15-30ml (1-2tbsp) apricot jam

Icing sugar in a sugar shaker

Edible glue

EQUIPMENT

Small rolling pin

Pastry brush

Cake smoother

Sable paintbrush: no. 2 (SK)

1cm (³/₈"), 2cm (³/₄") and 5cm (2") circle cutters

METHOD

1. Brush the top of each cupcake with a little apricot jam using the pastry brush. Roll out the white sugarpaste and cut circles to cover the top of each cake using the largest circle cutter. Smooth around the outside edge of each with your fingertip.

2. For the paw prints, roll out the coloured sugarpaste as thinly as possible, one colour at a time, and cut out a circle for the heel imprint using the 2cm (³/₄") circle cutter. Stretch this circle slightly and then stick in place using a little edible glue. Use the smaller circle cutter for the three toe imprints across the top. Press the cake smoother down onto the surface to smooth out any dimples.

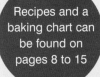
Recipes and a baking chart can be found on pages 8 to 15

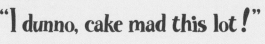
"I dunno, cake mad this lot!"

Templates

Wallace

pages 38-40

Enlarge template by 141%

Gromit

pages 41-43

Enlarge template by 141%

Anti-pesto Van

pages 48-53

WINDOW
(+ REVERSE)

BACK WINDOW

BONNET

FRONT WINDSCREEN

Templates actual size

Tea Time

pages 64-68

CHAIR BACK

CHAIR SEAT

Templates actual size

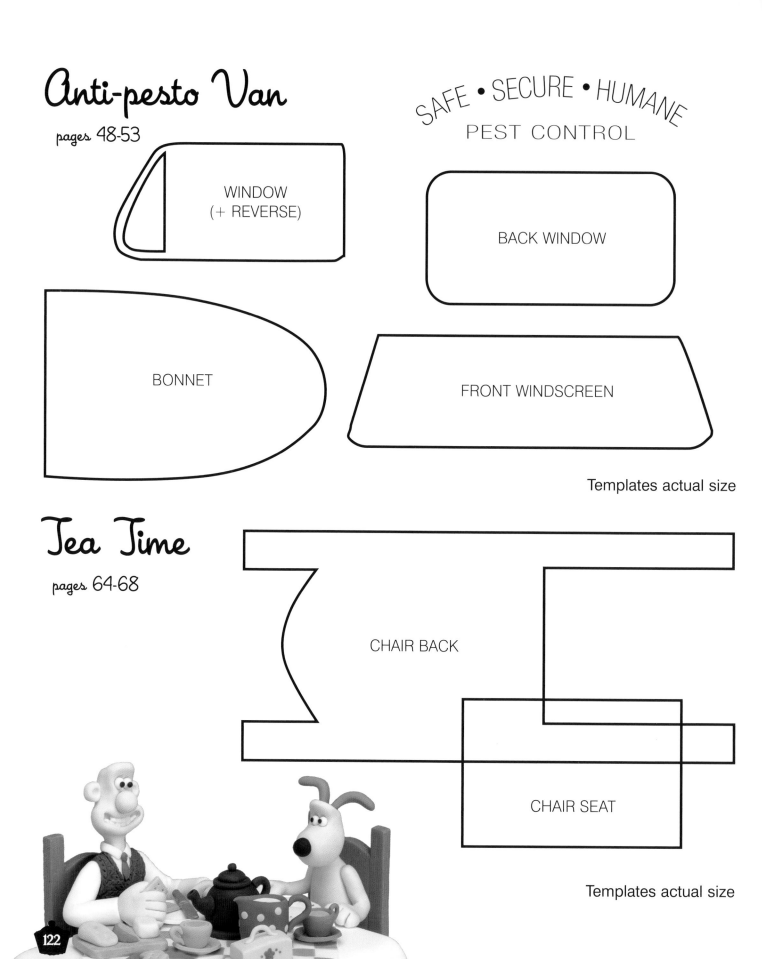

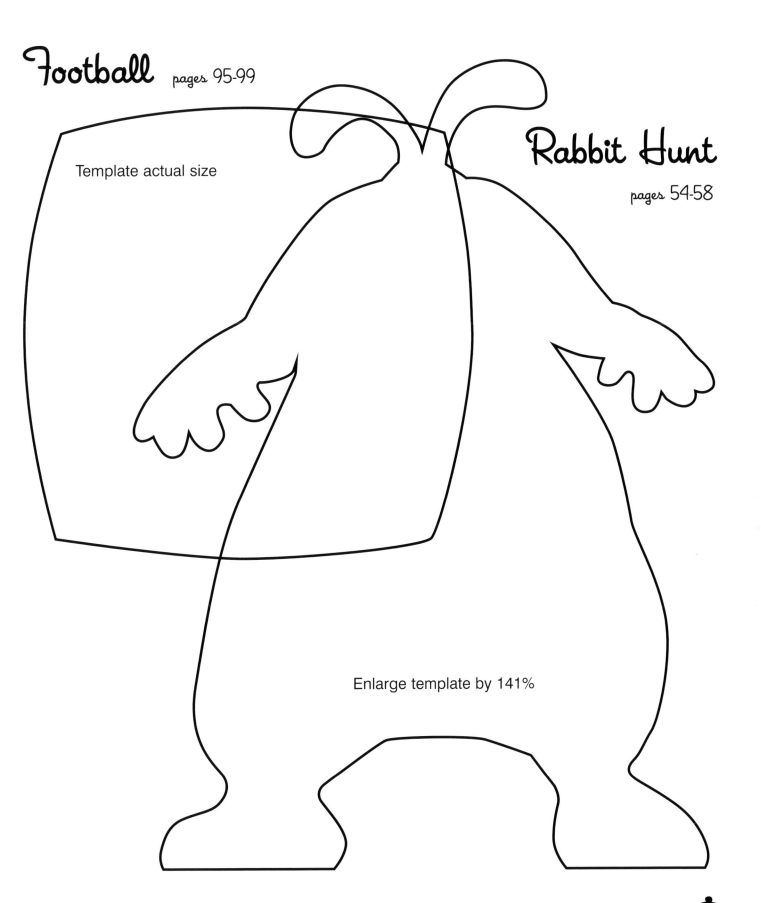

Football pages 95-99

Template actual size

Rabbit Hunt

pages 54-58

Enlarge template by 141%

Mini Cakes   pages 82-85

Templates actual size

Pop Art   pages 79-81

Template actual size

Mini Cakes pages 82-85

Templates actual size

Pop Art

Template actual size

Suppliers

Shops

UK

Jane Asher Party Cakes

24 Cale Street
London SW3 3QU
Tel: 020 7584 6177
Fax: 020 7584 6179
Website: www.jane-asher.co.uk

Pipedreams

2 Bell Lane
Eton Wick
Berkshire
Tel: 01753 865682

Squires Kitchen Sugarcraft (SK)

Squires House
3 Waverley Lane
Farnham
Surrey
GU9 8BB
Tel: 0845 22 55 67 1/2 (from UK)
+44 (0)1252 711749 (from overseas)
E-mail: info@squires-group.co.uk
Websites: www.squires-shop.com
www.squiresschool.co.uk

Sugar Celebrations

37 Faringdon Road
Swindon
Wiltshire
SN1 5AR
Tel: 01793 513549
and
80 Westgate Street
Gloucester
GL1 2NZ
Tel: 01452 308848
E-mail: girls@sugarcelebrations.com
Website: www.sugarcelebrations.com

AUSTRALIA

Cakedeco

Shop 7
Port Phillip Arcade
228 Flinders Street
Melbourne
Australia
Tel: +61 (0) 3 9654 5335
E-mail: cakedeco@optusnet.com.au

Iced Affair

53 Church St
Camperdown
NSW 2050
Australia
Tel: +61 (0) 2 9519 3679
E-mail: icedaffair@iprimus.com.au
Website: www.icedaffair.com

Suzy Q Cake Decorating Centre

Shop 4
372 Keilor Road
Niddrie
Victoria 3042
Australia
Tel: +61 (0) 3 9379 2275

BRAZIL

Boloarte

Rua Enes De Souza, 35 - Tijuca
Rio De Janeiro - RJ- CEP 20521-210
BRASIL
Tel: (55-21) 2288 7736 / 2238 9332
E-mail: cursos@boloarte.com.br
Website: www.boloarte.com.br

THE NETHERLANDS

Planet Cake®

Zuidplein 117
3083 CN
Rotterdam
The Netherlands
Tel: +31 (0)10 290 91 30
E-mail: info@cake.nl
Website: www.cake.nl

SWEDEN

Tårtdecor

Bultgatan 14
442 40 KUNGÄLV
Svierge
Tel: +46 303 514 70
E-mail: info@tartdecor.se
Website: www.tartdecor.se

Manufacturers and Distributors

UK

Confectionery Supplies

Unit 11a, b and c
Foley Trading Estate
Hereford
HR1 2SF
Tel: 01432 371451
029 2037 2161 (mail order)
E-mail: kclements@btinternet.com
Website: www.confectionerysupplies.co.uk

Guy, Paul & Co. Ltd.

Unit 10, The Business Centre
Corinium Industrial Estate
Raans Road
Amersham
Buckinghamshire
HP6 6FB
Tel: 01494 432121
E-mail: sales@guypaul.co.uk
Website: www.guypaul.co.uk

Renshaw

Crown Street
Liverpool
L8 7RF
E-mail: enquiries@renshaw-nbf.co.uk
Website: www.renshaw-nbf.co.uk
Manufacturers of Regalice and marzipan.

Squires Group

Squires House
3 Waverley Lane
Farnham
Surrey
GU9 8BB
Tel: 0845 22 55 67 1/2 (from UK)
+44 (0)1252 711749 (from overseas)
E-mail: info@squires-group.co.uk
Websites: www.squires-group.co.uk
www.cakesandsugarcraft.co.uk
www.squires-exhibition.co.uk

USA

Caljava International School of Cake Decorating and Sugar Craft

19519 Business Center Drive
Northridge, CA 91324 - USA
Tel: +1 818 718 2707
Fax: +1 818 718 2715
E-mail: caljava@aol.com
Website: cakevisions.com

Beryl's Cake Decorating & Pastry Supplies

PO Box 1584
N. Springfield, VA
USA
Tel: +1 800 488 2749
Website: www.beryls.com

Guilds

The British Sugarcraft Guild

Wellington House
Messeter Place
London
SE9 5DP
Tel: 020 8859 6943
Website: www.bsguk.org

"I'm just crackers about cheese!"